*mortal saints and
immortal callings*

mortal saints and immortal callings

VOCATION IN THE LIVES OF THE SAINTS

A'DORA PHILLIPS

PARACLETE PRESS
BREWSTER, MASSACHUSETTS

2006   First Printing

Copyright © 2006 by A'Dora Phillips

ISBN 1-55725-434-6

Library of Congress Cataloging-in-Publication Data
Phillips, A'Dora.
Mortal saints & immortal callings : vocation in the lives of the saints /
A'Dora Phillips.
    p.cm.
Includes bibliographical references.
ISBN 1-55725-434-6
1. Christian saints—Biography. 2. Vocation—Christianity. I. Title:
Mortal saints and immortal callings. II. Title.
BR1710.P45 2006
270.092'2—dc22   2005033055

10 9 8 7 6 5 4 3 2 1

Published by Paraclete Press
Brewster, Massachusetts
www.paracletepress.com
Printed in the United States of America.

For Brian

contents

*mortal saints and
immortal callings*

1
mortal saints and immortal callings

SAINT JOAN OF ARC AND
SAINT MARGARET OF ANTIOCH

When you saw the voice coming to you, was there any light?
There was light all about, and so there should be!

ST. JOAN OF ARC ANSWERING HER JUDGES

FOR ME, AS FOR SO MANY OTHERS, JOAN OF ARC WAS MY
first encounter with the transformative power of a
human driven by divine impulse, and she came to me, of
all places, via the television set. I was four years old and
living in Ohio that year with my mother and sisters. It
was the early seventies, and on that particular day, I sat
alone in our living room watching a black and white
film about Joan of Arc's life on what would be the last
amniotic day of my childhood.

I remember nothing about the film except the end—the end that would have receded with so many other events into the depths of my unconscious were it not for the most inhumane conflagration of her final hour. "Her career," wrote Vita Sackville-West so appropriately, "if it was to be rounded off into the unity which it dramatically demanded, must end in an early and tragic death." Certainly for me had she not burned, she would never have risen from my childhood amnesia. Yet the screen filled with flames, licking up and around her darkening silhouette, and I realized that she had been condemned to die a terrible death simply for doing as she believed God had directed her to do.

Something within me became very still and quiet—as if things were moving aside to make room for new life. This is, I suppose, what consciousness is when it emerges in a child—the first tendrils of individual awareness gaining the light of day; the deep water and dark earth of childhood sinking away. I was not then old enough to understand that some people stand alone in defense of their calling, guarding it with their lives, their courage an affirmation to those of us who give credence to the spirit and things beyond rational comprehension. But I nevertheless in some way comprehended the core of her story. Though very young, I was old enough to understand in simplest terms that Joan of Arc had been called, had been brave, and had been sacrificed. I was old enough to sense that there was injustice and evil in the world. As children often are, I was old (or young) enough to identify with her suffering.

mortal saints and immortal callings

It's astonishing how early we begin looking for models of behavior to help us negotiate our way in the world, and, for me, Joan's steadfast courage penetrated my heart at a formative time. I spent many years after seeing that film searching for answers to questions that were in some form born that day when I was four—questions about spiritual life, about receiving a calling, about battling to overcome injustice in the world. It wouldn't be an exaggeration to say that my growing consciousness crystallized around the questions and images Joan of Arc planted in my mind. She inspired me with the belief that I, that all of us, are meant to undertake some special work in life and must remain faithful to it come what may. As my life plays out, I realize that Joan of Arc became a guide to me at that time of my youth, as Saints Catherine and Margaret were to Joan.

I am not alone in my admiration of Joan of Arc. More than five hundred years, over half a millennium, have passed since she was lashed to a stake one spring morning in the old market square in Rouen, France, and set afire. Many generations have lived and died. Yet in her name, books continue to be written, movies made, prayers said, questions asked, and courage called upon.

Even in this, our age of reason, when many of us are less able to believe in the miracles of her life (surviving a leap from a tower, a dove flying from her mouth as she burned, her heart remaining whole while the rest of her body lay in ashes), we hold on to her faith and courage as a miracle. Even in our age of skepticism, when we question the voices she claimed to have heard and propose that she may have been schizophrenic, we revere her conviction of purpose. And even in this age of cynicism when it's suggested that she might have grown vengeful and power hungry as she sought to carry out God's work, it's impossible for most of us to dismiss her as having been blood-thirsty and filled with hubris.

Her life, instead, manifests what we so often feel in our hearts to be true: that each of us is given special gifts and the spiritual grace we need to employ them.

For many years I have striven to become a painter, and in the course of this pursuit, more than thirty years after my encounter with Joan, a second saint stepped into my life, as numinous and unexpected as that day when I was four. I had traveled from New York to France, hoping to be allowed to study with a master painter and teacher, only to find myself turned away when I arrived. I left France and went to Florence, Italy, to visit another art academy, only to find that all of their places for the upcoming spring had already been filled with other students who were hungry for training.

Alone with my hopes and desires, and questioning the choices I had made in my life, I walked to the Uffizi Galleries along the bank of the Arno River through the cobbled streets of Florence. Very little of the centuries-old color and grandeur of the city captured my attention. I passed the musicians and street artists who lined the colonnaded steps up to the foot of the main entrance of

mortal saints and immortal callings

the museum, after standing in line for an hour, ascended the staircase to the room displaying selections from the Uffizi's master drawing collection. Not aware that my mind and spirit were elsewhere, lost in the turbulent waters of my inner self, I stopped in front of a pencil sketch by Pontormo, a sixteenth-century Italian painter whose delicate drawings I greatly admire. As in the past when I'd seen his small works on display at the Metropolitan Museum in New York, I studied the sensitive exactitude of his line work, but my disappointment imposed itself and I, little able to appreciate what I saw, passed unmoved.

With hardly a glance, I climbed the last flight of stairs and entered the great corridor of the Uffizi, replete with exquisite Roman and Hellenistic marbles. Light washed over them from the clerestory windows, their views looking over the red-tiled Florentine rooftops, billowing clouds of rising pigeons, spring blue sky, and Tuscan hills. It was the first time I had been there, and, oh how beautiful it was! But I felt none of what I saw, lived nothing of what I experienced.

I began walking through the galleries, arranged in chronological order starting with the thirteenth century. I went past work by the masters Cimabue, Giotto, and Fra Angelico. Past Botticelli's *Birth of Venus*, da Vinci's unfinished *Adoration of the Magi*, Raphael, del Sarto, and Pontormo. Sometimes I paused momentarily to glance at something, though I knew not what. My mind full of idle thoughts, my mood dark, at no point was I conscious of the miracle of creation that surrounded me. It was, instead, a day of idle thought. *How strange they've hung that painting so high. I wonder if the room is dark to preserve the paintings. It seems the color in the restored work is too brilliant and lacks depth.*

Entering room 28, where the Titians are housed, I walked past a painting of a woman by another sixteenth-century artist, Jacopo Palma the Elder. *Such a strange expression on her face*, I thought in a fleeting way, though I didn't stop to consider why. Several of Titian's portraits followed, the illuminated brilliance of *Flora* (shyly offering flowers), the sensuous languor of *Venus of Urbino*. My eyes traced the corners of the room as I spun a quick pirouette preparing to leave, when, in spite of myself, my conscious mind was awakened for the first time that day by the presence of a woman whose beauty I can only describe as earthen—full lips, ample figure, and strong neck—in three-quarter view, her head thrown back, her upper body suffused with light.

Her facial expression was that of someone frozen in the act of crying out. Her upward-turned eyes, swollen and still glimmering with tears, spoke of resolution and a will to not be overcome. Her arms stretched outward, the palm of her right hand facing up toward someone or something beyond. The arm was sturdy but the hand itself small, the only part of her that appeared defenseless. In her left hand, she held a palm frond, a symbol of martyrdom. A beautiful mesmerizing arc of light washed over her figure, from where the young woman's head was thrown back down to where the folds of her robe began to disappear in darkness.

My eyes traveled from the light that illuminated her face and shoulders down into the dark corner of the painting, where a nameless creature ascended toward her. Its wide-open jaws, which is all Titian depicted of the beast, pushed up from oily darkness. The beast was mainly in shadow, but menacing shards of light glanced off the ribs of the roof of its mouth, off its fangs, its lower gums, and the tip of its tongue. What struck me first, what transfixed me, was the woman's strength of purpose in the face of terror. A dark force had intruded upon her, but the woman in the painting neither turned away in fear, nor cowered back from it. Although I intuitively knew that she understood the gravity of the situation, she altogether refused to succumb, instead remaining steadfast in the presence of danger. Her absolute faith, I sensed, was the secret of her strength.

I did not know as I first took in the painting that I was looking at Titian's depiction of Margaret of Antioch, who, along with St. Catherine and the archangels Michael and Gabriel, had guided Joan of Arc. Today we question whether or not she actually ever existed, but during Titian's time Margaret was a steady presence in the daily life of the people, a "Holy Helper"—one of fourteen saints whose assistance could be invoked with confidence during times of adversity.

A Roman martyr, Margaret was born in Antioch of pagan parents, but shortly after her birth, her mother sent her to be raised by a Christian nurse outside the city walls. She grew into a beautiful and devout young woman and, while tending sheep in the fields one day, caught the eye of Olibrius, a rich lord who worshiped pagan gods. He sent his men with the message that he wanted to either marry her or take her as his mistress (the former if she was of noble, the latter if she was of common birth). Confident of getting his own way, he prematurely boasted to his friends of the fine clothes she would wear for him.

However, when Olibrius's messengers told her of the riches awaiting her, she remained unmoved and refused to meet their lord.

Olibrius ordered her brought before him. Speaking gently at first, he asked her to tell him her name, then flirtatiously he asked if she "really" believed in Christ. She was not swayed by gentle words and would not consent to be his wife, so he cast her into prison for the night. In the morning, he asked if she'd reconsidered and would prefer the kingdoms of Asia and Antioch, the best meat of the land, fine clothes, and wealth, to the coldness of a cell. She repeated her faith in the truth of Christ and implored him to replace his stone gods with the eternal love of which she spoke. While some Roman suitors were converted by similar pleas from the virgins they tried to woo, Olibrius ordered his men to beat Margaret until blood ran from her body, ordered them to tear the flesh from her bones.

"Will you not have pity on your flesh?" he asked when he saw the fortitude with which she withstood her torture. "Will you not have mercy on yourself?"

To Olibrius, Margaret said that though he might have power over her flesh and bone, he had no power to take her soul. Or, as expressed in the powerful rhythms of the Middle English couplet used as a charm during childbirth: *Though thou have posté of my flesshe and boon,/ To take from Cryste my soule power haste thou noone.*

This assertion of her own ultimate freedom from anything that might imprison her in the material world, only served to inflame her suitor's rage, and, once again, she was cast behind bars. The common iconography that depicts her with the dragon originates from the three days she spent incarcerated. It is here that the beast appeared in front of her, swallowed her, and was burst asunder by the power of her faith, and it is here that an equally hideous demon materialized in his place. This devil, too, she overcame, binding him with her headdress. Helpless and prostrate before her, the creature revealed that, among other things, wherever Satan knew of a woman whose child was not yet born, he went there to do her harm.

When Olibrius finally had Margaret led to the outskirts of town to be beheaded, she beseeched Christ to allow her to intercede on behalf of women in childbirth, a request that it appears was granted.

Years before, I'd read the story of Margaret in *The Golden Legend*, a medieval compilation of the lives of the saints. At the time, her life had seemed no different from that of all the other young Roman virgin martyrs: beautiful, innocent, faithful to Christ, lusted after, tortured, and killed. I had not seen the point of the story, but now I better understood both the message of her martyrdom and why Margaret, who stood up against patriarchy, would most obviously have come to the aid of Joan, who stood up against the forces of church and state. There might be another reason, as well that Margaret, patroness of childbirth, appeared as a guide to Joan. In following our callings in this world we give birth to our lives sometimes amid pain and danger. Perhaps Margaret stayed beside Joan to ensure that in the long hours of her labor she would not falter.

As I stared into Titian's vision of Margaret, all I could see was light—the palpable illumination of the world which I loved, the physical beauty of the world I wanted to learn to capture in paint, the spiritual matter that helps us all to live with greater dignity, charity, and freedom. On the surface of this painting, the darkness lay heavy at the bottom, while the light streamed in from above, filling the abyss. It is testament to Titian's genius that he, who lived in the sixteenth century, an age that revered the presence of Margaret, had managed, with flakes of pigment and a vast experience of the world, to convey the essence of her message to us: remain steadfast and believe; our souls cannot be taken.

As if a veil had been lifted from my eyes, I looked anew around the room. It was Judith I'd glimpsed when I'd first stepped into the gallery, the Jewish heroine who

mortal saints and immortal callings

delivered her native city from the onslaught of Holofernes by entering his camp and beheading him as he slept; cradling the general's head in her arms, she beseeched us with wild eyes to understand what she had done. I turned from her to Titian's *Portrait of Francesco Maria della Rovere*, an aging knight in shiny mirrored armor. A spiritual self-portrait on the part of Titian, perhaps, the knight's armor reflected bits and pieces of the world, while his dark eyes absorbed it. He, too, surveyed me, surveyed us all, from the painting, world-weary and sorry, weathered but wise. From the draft of his experience, he seemed to beg the question: "What did you expect, after all? That things were going to be easy?"

There was no difference, I suddenly saw, between the challenges I felt in Florence and the beast in Titian's painting. As with Margaret, a dark force had intruded upon my life, but a crucial difference lay in how I reacted to it as compared to Margaret, for in the face of difficulty I had begun to falter. The true question was not where I would study but whether I had the faith to persevere in making real what I desired for myself in the world.

It is not that the saints teach and instruct us about goodness and godliness and loftiness; or, at least, that's not the whole of it. Rather, as beauty is said to attract evil, so their timeless callings do as well, making manifest to our eyes that from which we must protect ourselves. Just as the individual variety of the saints' lives and vocations inspire us to search and hold to the uniqueness of our own visions, so their many and varied struggles provide examples of the many and varied shapes adversity may take in our own lives. The abuse of patriarchy and other forms of authority; social injustice; the skepticism, judgment, indifference, or persecution of others; interior attitudes and expectations that mire us in darkness—such are the corners where the mighty dragon lurks.

The acts of Margaret, for centuries one of the Church's most beloved saints, were written once upon long strips of parchment and wrapped around the bellies of women in labor. In the long hours of delivery, intoned within smoky, candle-lit chambers, the rhymes and rhythms of her story, so easy for people to remember, welcomed new life into safety.

How little time we are given to be of this mortal flesh! How essential it is that we live on and struggle and love and lose and gain and learn on this earthly plane, giving what we can, seeking guidance, remaining steadfast, confronting difficulty with courage, believing in the importance of following our callings, and bearing down to see them born.

2
transformation: ascent along the uphill road

SAINT FRANCIS OF ASSISI

...[F]or me Saint Francis is the model of the dutiful man, the man who by means of ceaseless, supremely cruel struggle succeeds in fulfilling our highest obligation, something higher even than morality or truth or beauty: the obligation to transubstantiate the matter which God entrusted to us, and turn it into spirit.

NIKOS KAZANTZAKIS

A CHAPEL DEVOTED TO FRANCIS STOOD A FEW MILES FROM where I lived in France—situated on a hill overlooking a valley, fifty yards from a spring, amid pine trees and scrubby little oaks scattering the ridge along one of the old pilgrimage roads to Santiago de Compostela in Spain. The one small room was always open, a few wooden chairs, a couple of candles on the altarpiece, sometimes an offering of flowers, leaves, or a stone left behind by a visitor. When a child from the area had run away from home, the police knew that he or she would inevitably seek out this refuge, trying to sleep away the torture of what had driven them out to mingle with the spooky sound of white barn owls and the skitter of mice. It's impossible not to think of the young Francis in relation to the boys and girls who shelter themselves there today, Francis who requested refuge from the priest at the church of San Damiano when, as a young man, he realized his spiritual calling was at odds with the materialistic values of his father.

I visited this chapel only once after sunset, biking up on a cold evening with a friend to bury an owl I'd found on the road, though I went there frequently by myself during the day—sometimes to paint landscapes from the road overlooking the ravine and sometimes to sit inside, listening to silence filtered through the hum of wind and stone.

Always when I would go to this refuge I would walk to the still pool where underground spring water collected on the surface just a few yards distant, its own little stone shelter piled up lovingly and carefully around it. I'd stoop down and look into the dark waters, knowing that it was no accident that the chapel up the hill had been built in close proximity to this deep and mysterious spring, site and source of a miracle or two, no doubt, now forgotten in the buried bones of the past.

The mulch of dead leaves lay still on its glassy surface, tendrils of soft growth barely discernible within its yellow-green depths. Vague shadows cast by the afternoon sun stretched and dissolved into its depths. Why this desire to go over to the spring and look into its darkness? Why this desire to ruffle the surface, just a touch, and dip my hand in to cup cool water, surprised to find that that which had looked so dark and murky from afar would appear so clear and clean in my palm? Dark and light seem so often dependent, one upon the other, and the dark waters of the spring frightened me—much as looking into the fathomless black of a well would—and yet they seemed most holy. If only as a metaphor, its shadowy recesses seemed as important to its healing touch as the moment its cool waters revealed their pureness in the palm of my hand.

But what does this have to do with vocation and Francis of Assisi, to whom that place was consecrated?

To my mind, the circumstances of this chapel are emblematic of Francis's gift to us. Wherever we may go to pay homage to this man, it is as that chapel on the hill—a pure white tranquility drawn from the deep and mysterious wellspring of his life.

Perhaps no saint better exemplifies the dark waters of the human condition than Francis. Yet with no saint, I think, are we more compelled in our day to turn away from the broad experience of his life and its implications on our vocations, our callings. It is as if we are fearful that the *shadowy* aspects might take away the relief that we seek. We purchase our food in sanitized Styrofoam, rush our sick and wounded and dying away and out of sight. In like kind, we honor Francis for perceiving what we now call the "Gaia" of existence (his recognition of the "primordial source of all things," as Bonaventure, his first official biographer relates), averting our gaze from the severe penances he brought upon himself in his effort to break down the boundaries of his body and mind.

We revere Francis as the one who called for politeness, economy, and care in the way we should walk the earth, turning away from the extremes of his nature (stripping to his underwear, dragging himself to the stone where criminals were punished, and climbing on top of it to preach nearly naked in the winter cold). We delight in his having addressed sermons to sparrows, overlooking the fact that he did this because he was sometimes left alone, ridiculed by his community. We abbreviate his stooping to kiss a leper on the lips, as if it were an anecdotal insanity.

There are times when we want to think of Francis as a child. In this very complicated world where we are compromised in our daily lives, surrounded by corruption, and we struggle with the presence of cynicism, Francis offers hope that we can live adult lives sustained by the simplicity of a child's mind. Indeed, once when we were young in this world, we spoke to the sparrows too. We raised our arms out to our sides and swooped about, and we called the birds our sisters. We embraced *sister water*, *brother fire*, our *sister, mother earth*, the *colored flowers*, *green plants* and *sister, bodily death*, as did he near the end of his life in his *Canticle of the Sun*.

Before we knew of physics and biology, we understood, as Francis did, that everything was alive and that we were all part of the great unbroken chain of existence connected to God, gendered and engendered with purpose—sun and moon, stones and trees, birds and humans of all sorts, fire and water, earth and air, and all. And in our search for wholeness, for holiness, for connection to the voices that guide our paths in this world, it is easy to look at Francis and think, *Oh, to have remained a child like he.*

It is for this reason that I cup the dark waters and search for the fullness of his vocation.

There appears to be a gentleness in the way God prepared Francis for the hard work he was to do in life, revealing to him the nascent beginnings of his calling in a dream. As Bonaventure writes in his biography, God showed Francis in this dream "a large and splendid palace full of military weapons emblazoned with the insignia of Christ's cross. . . . [W]hen Francis asked to whom these belonged, he received an answer from heaven that all these things were for him and his knights." Initially interpreting the dream literally to mean that he would have great prosperity, Francis set off to a nearby town to offer his services as a knight to a count there. He'd not traveled far, though, when God addressed him, explaining to Francis that he'd misunderstood his dream, which had a spiritual meaning, not a literal one. Francis interrupted his journey and returned home.

Up to that point in his life, with the exception of an "openhanded compassion for the poor," Francis had lived the life of a typical, well-to-do boy of that time, selling cloth at the market for his father and carousing with friends. After returning to Assisi, however, he prepared himself for God's work, beginning with trying to overcome the instinctive drives of his nature. The sight of lepers filled him with horror and revulsion, for instance, so, one day, upon seeing a man covered with leprous sores, he dismounted his horse and ran to kiss him—the first significant action that signaled the profound spiritual transformation that was already underway and would unfold throughout the remainder of his life.

By virtue of his new interests, he began to distance himself from friends, "to seek out solitary places" and to pray "incessantly with unutterable groanings." He wore torn and ragged clothes and visited the houses of lepers to distribute alms and to care for them, kissing their hands and mouths. He distributed his possessions to beggars and assisted the less fortunate priests at the small churches around Assisi. He made a pilgrimage to the shrine of Peter, where he gave his own clothes to the neediest beggar at the door of church, dressing in turn in the man's rags and mixing with the poor.

While he was in the crumbling church of San Damiano one day, a voice from the cross finally told him of his calling. Three times, this voice said: "Francis, go and repair my house, which, as you see, is falling completely into ruin." With his characteristic and lovable misunderstanding, Francis failed to grasp that God was calling on him to repair the spiritual foundation of the church. With the equally characteristic enthusiasm of his good will, he raided his father's store and rushed off to a nearby town to sell the cloth he'd taken, as well as the horse he was riding. Knowing that Francis's parents were angry, the parish priest wouldn't accept the money Francis tried to give him from the transaction, but did allow the young man to stay with him rather than force him to return to a home that was increasingly opposed to his burgeoning vocation.

Hearing that Francis had taken refuge at San Damiano, his father set out with the intent of bringing him back home. Receiving a premonition that his father was on his way, and fearful of his wrath, Francis hid in a secret pit for several days until finally he gained the courage to return to Assisi and confront his father about what he'd done.

Consider the narrative of Francis's life as it unfolded up to this point. A merchant's son in his late teens, selling cloth in the marketplace, had an extraordinarily vibrant dream. Convinced that he was meant to become a knight, he set out to commend himself to a nearby lord, returning home soon after, as if in failure. He openly began to change, laying bare his soul, the hidden riches of his spirit, to people who'd known him his entire life as Pietro Bernardone's son. Imagine: the failed journey, the watchful eyes of family and friends, the wagging tongues as he was drawn to kiss the sores of lepers, rip apart his clothes, and steal cloth from his father in order to carry out the command of a voice that spoke to him from the cross in San Damiano, a voice no one else had heard.

We might condemn such actions and beliefs as that of a madman, or at minimum dismiss them with a shrug, as if knowing that one day he would outgrow them.

It was as hard for people then as it is now to believe in the eccentricity of his calling. As he walked down the streets of Assisi toward his childhood home to face the consequences of his actions—"unkempt" and completely changed from who he'd been before—his neighbors lined up, and, thinking him mad, insulted him as he passed, hurling stones and garbage. Hearing the commotion, his father ran out and grabbed hold of Francis, dragging him into the house—"not to save him but to destroy him."

Having no native sympathy for his son whatsoever, his father never stopped to ask Francis what was the source of the reason for his strange behavior. Rather, he beat him, belittled him, and chained him up. He brought a lawsuit against his son and the two of them ended up before the bishop of Assisi. There, in one of the many dramatic gestures of his life, Francis not only renounced his family possessions but stripped himself naked before the assembled crowd and divested himself of his paternity: "Until now I have called you father here on earth," he said, "but now I can say without reservation, 'Our Father who art in heaven,' since I have placed all my treasure and all my hope in him."

Breaking from the chrysalis of his past, Francis became the son of God rather than the son of his earthly father, and he set out, son and man, to continue his journey. It was 1206. Four years had passed since his first vision, and he was twenty-two years old.

I wonder how many of us suffer to some degree the alienation that Francis felt, this dissociation from cultural and contemporary norms, the need for change, the nagging awareness that something is not right. I also wonder how few of us would leave our families behind, walk away from earthly goods, remove our clothes and stand naked in front of the world, our words delineating a spiritual and physical departure from our earlier selves? It's hard to do such a thing, and yet this was just the first of the many hard things Francis would do.

After divesting himself of his earthly father, he lived as a penitent hermit, caring for lepers and helping to repair several ruined churches. He began to attract followers, and in 1208, began preaching publicly, donning the simple brown tunic and hood of a shepherd. In 1209, he drafted a primitive rule based on a few texts from the Gospel and took it to Rome with a small group of "friars minor," as they called themselves, securing the approval of Pope Innocent III for the first of three Franciscan orders. Emphasizing the holiness and "wealth" of poverty, he and his followers fanned out in small groups through central Italy, supporting themselves through simple manual labor and preaching to those around them.

Francis's journey took him to the Middle East, where he hoped to convert Muslims but instead faced the abuses of the Crusades, returning to Italy, after many miles of pilgrimage, to attend to a crisis in his growing order. Under pressure from church officials, he resigned as head of the Franciscans in 1220, leaving it to others to shape as they would the order he had founded. Having pursued his spiritual aims at the cost of his body and material comfort, with his health now failing, he spent long periods praying alone on Mount La Verna, where he received the stigmata, the replicas of the wounds of Christ in his own body. Nearly blind, body aged beyond his years, he approached his death at forty-two, completely bare and unadorned before God.

We could contemplate for a very long time the traumas, dreams, losses, hopes, desires, miracles, perceptions, and joys of Francis's life. His stories and their messages now flow with ease across the centuries, the emotional torture softened by the grace of the holy fool: cheerful boldness and generosity that sprung from the belief that he had nothing to lose—neither reputation, friends, family, life, health, nor innocence itself. With everything to gain, he offered friendship and alms to all, fearless of his well running dry. He was, as Bonaventure wrote, a polished mirror, slick and brilliant, reflecting holiness.

Though Francis was always a popular saint, his cult blossomed dramatically in the twentieth century among

Christians and non-believers alike. From the beginning of this revival of interest in his life and values, writers sought to remind an idealizing public of the profound physical and spiritual depths of his lived experience. The early twentieth-century British writer G. K. Chesterton came of age in tandem with an entire generation discovering the beauty of Francis's message amid the horror and conflict of war. In *Saint Francis of Assisi*, Chesterton explains that he wrote his book in part to remind us of the depths and complexities of Francis's calling to practice ascetical spirituality, which the modern age, as he saw it, wished to dismiss as an "accident."

The Greek writer, thinker, and pilgrim Nikos Kazantzakis was another writer of that time to dramatize Francis's life. In his novel *Saint Francis*, which he dedicated to the Alsatian theologian and medical missionary Albert Schweitzer ("the Saint Francis of Our Era"), he tells of wanting to "match the saint's life to his myth," to offer a fuller portrait of the man than was generally conveyed at the time. Told from the point-of-view of Francis's friar Brother Leo, Kazantzaki depicts the extremes of struggle and sacrifice that attended Francis's ascension to sainthood, attempting to evoke the reality of a life lived so close to the earth, of Francis's spiritual sufferings over the brutality of the Crusades, of the ordeal of having his order overtaken, and of the disintegration of his body, which he called "Brother Ass."

In Kazantzakis's novel, Francis guides Leo, obviously the author's alter ego, who in turn tells us as readers what

Francis has taught him. The lessons are difficult ones for Leo to embrace, as the way of life called for by Francis often seems inimical to human instinct. It is painful for Leo to watch the man he loves, Francis, the man who calls himself "a clay lamp made from the soil," disintegrate physically before his eyes, difficult for him to believe that so much sacrifice and effort are required of us. Yet he tells us in the end that he learned many things from Francis that proved to be true: among other things, that there is no road to follow, only an abyss into which we must jump. He learns that God will tell us that He wants that which we do not, that He loves that which we hate, and that we will never have given enough until we break in two. He tells us that it's impossible for a person "to leave his donkey on the plain to graze in rich pastures, while his soul, weightless and insensible to hunger and cold, climbed the mountain." And, finally, Brother Leo says that Francis tells us this:

> The caterpillar is me, Sister Clara, and you and also all the sisters listening to me, and every person who crawls upon earth. Good God, what feats this poor wretched caterpillar must accomplish before being transformed into a butterfly! Struggle and more struggle, my sisters, ascent along the uphill road, extreme suffering; and purity, love, poverty, hunger, nakedness, tears—all these are required! . . .

3

finding
true center

SAINT TERESA OF ÁVILA

When I was among the pleasures of the world, I was
saddened by the memory of what I owed to God, and my
worldly affections disturbed me when I was with God.
A battle like this is so painful that I do not know how
I managed to endure it...for so many years.

ST. TERESA OF ÁVILA

THE BAROQUE SCULPTOR GIANLORENZO BERNINI'S *ECSTASY*
of Teresa at the Cornaro Chapel of Santa Maria della
Vittoria in Rome invites us to view an intimate moment
between God and the great Spanish mystic who spent her
life poised on the borderland between heaven and earth. In
this sculpture, framed theatrically for over three centuries
by four columns of blue-black stone, Bernini chose to
honor Teresa by depicting one of her most famous
visions. Of this vision Teresa records the following in her
autobiography, written when she was forty-seven:

Beside me, on the left, appeared an angel in bodily form. . . . not tall, but short and very beautiful; and his face was so aflame that he appeared to be one of the highest rank of angels. . . . In his hands I saw a great golden spear, and at the iron tip there appeared to be a point of fire. This he plunged into my heart several times so that it penetrated to my entrails. When he drew it out, I thought he was drawing them out with it and he left me utterly consumed by the great love of God.

The angel written of by Teresa, suspended in milky-white, polished marble, has, in Bernini's piece, withdrawn the spear and looks down upon the swooning saint, head tilted to the side, an expression of playful love on his face. Teresa's figure, slender and aquiline, remains a paragon of feminine beauty even by today's standards. Her head arches back, eyes closed, lips parted, a nun's cowl framing her classically balanced features. A thick hand as that of a worker dangles from the sleeve of her ample robes; a shoeless foot reveals itself from beneath the drapes of her habit, a symbol of her place as the foundress of the Discalced Carmelites. Her hands and feet are of the earth; her face and elegant drape of body—more folds of cloth than bone—float in weightless suspension.

When the sculpture was unveiled in 1652, Bernini was accused of dragging Teresa through the dirt, of "prostituting" her, turning her into "a Venus." In Victorian times,

Stendhal and others criticized the work as "unabashed eroticism."

But I believe, rather, that Teresa simply provided Bernini, as with so many others over the centuries, with the inspiration that allowed him to access the full potential of his creative vision. As if in a gesture of gratitude, his artistic intuition apprehended the unique calling of this woman and immortalized it in perpetuity. She was Spain's great female mystic; a Carmelite nun whose depth of prayer has rarely been equaled; a natural writer whose works, legendary in Spain, have been translated into languages the world over; a reformer and foundress of the Discalced Carmelites; a mentor to her nuns; and, since 1970, a Doctor of the Church. But her life as a nun, writer, reformer, and foundress was merely the surface fruit of the deeper labor she felt called to undertake, that being, to save her soul: to find her true center while torn between worldly affections and God.

A year after experiencing Bernini's master work, and desiring to understand his inspiration for such a magnificent piece, I began my first readings of Teresa's autobiography. From the first candid line of her narrative, the tone and tenor of her voice was that of a good friend—honest, down-to-earth, full of insight, and not without a little humor: "If I had not been so wicked it would have been a help to me that I had parents who were virtuous and feared God."

After reading several pages, I realized she was the guide I'd always longed to have. She had experienced a full life, and in writing about prayer and spiritual progress, she addressed my day-to-day existence on earth, putting words to invisible things, peppering her insights with priceless advice. Hold yourself in high esteem, she writes; understand what you have received so that you may "wake into love"; water the garden of your soul, laboriously, if need be (should the Lord not water it Himself), by pulling buckets from the well. Do not be afraid of your own thoughts; learn things through experience, not by books alone ("for it is strange what a difference there is between understanding a thing and subsequently knowing it by experience"); and seek out older, wiser people to direct you along your path.

She writes that "whatever the spirit may do, it does not escape from its solitude," that she learned about herself through interacting with others, that "tears gain everything," and that "cobwebs have to be brushed away from the memory." I could trust her unequivocally to speak the truth, a truth she discovered through living her own life of continual self-betterment, something she reminds us of periodically throughout her work: "I write this for the comfort of weak souls like myself, that they may never despair or lose their trust in God's greatness."

I am not alone in the feelings of intimacy and kinship I have toward the message she bears. Nearly everyone who goes to her seems to find in her a mentor, with some pertinent piece of guidance that helps them in their life. As Bernini so beautifully evoked, she put to form an archetypal calling we all share, that being to save ourselves, to bring ourselves closer to God, to actualize our gifts by marrying the often apparently divergent tendencies of our inner selves.

From Teresa of Ávila's birth to her death sixty-seven years later, she lived a life surrounded by a community that supported and loved her, even in times of struggle. "On Wednesday, the 28th of March, 1515, at 5:00 in the morning within half an hour or so of daybreak my daughter Teresa was born," her father records on the day on her birth, becoming her steadfast ally and protector. Teresa died on the feast of St. Francis in 1582, her head cradled in the arms of a Carmelite lay sister who served as Teresa's nurse-companion in the last years of her life. In the years between, she won the affection of nearly every man, woman, and child who came into contact with her. She earned the special love of God, as well, a vision she experienced in 1556 at the age of forty-one marking her "Mystical Betrothal" to Christ. So compelling was her influence that, disinterred after her death and found miraculously incorrupt, her body was dismembered by the faithful, who took away parts of it as relics.

The burgeoning vocational pull of this woman who would become, among other things, one of the greatest spiritual writers of all time seems in retrospect to have been evident even in the pastimes of her earliest childhood. She and her brother would read the lives of the saints together and dreamed of dying as the martyrs had. They built hermitages in the orchard next to their home and pretended to live as anchorites. She tells of giving alms when she could, trying to be alone when she said her prayers, and loving to build convents when she played with other little girls.

I'm reminded when I read Teresa's early reminiscences of an autobiography I once read by an elderly midwife from Alabama. Reflecting on the course of her vocation, she said she knew from an early age that she was called to care for people because, when she played with her dolls, she'd imagine they were sick, and she was there to make them feel better. Teresa's love of stories, which she claims eventually began to lead her astray, her preoccupation with the adventure rather than sanctity of religion, seem to me the beautiful foreshadowing of what she was to become.

When Teresa was twelve years old her mother died, precipitating, as she describes, the beginning of her descent into her sinful early years, out of which her vocational life was defined. As she entered adolescence, under the doting and tolerant eyes of her father, she indulged herself in many and varied transgressions, including the reading of books on chivalry, highly controversial for their romanticism. Spirited, intelligent, beautiful, charismatic, and perhaps a bit spoiled, Teresa liked to please others and craved attention. As with many of us in our teenage years, she was interested in gossip, fashion, and eliciting admiration. But most significantly, she reflects, and the one subject about which she remains uncharacteristically vague, she became interlaced in the lives of her "worldly" cousins, as she called them, particularly one from whom she learned, she says, "every kind of evil."

Even at the age of forty-seven as she wrote her autobiography, the memory of that relationship seemed to fill Teresa with shame, for the mortal sin of which she was to repent for many of the remaining years of her life emerged from their girlish tête-à-têtes. The vague and obscure hints she gives us as to what led her to live with such guilt have left to posterity's conjecture whether she did anything more than indulge her youthful vanity. It's been speculated that she engaged in an amorous affair, but ultimately we know only that Teresa was wracked with guilt and that her father sent her to an Augustinian convent where she would receive a "finishing" education in preparation for marriage.

She was sixteen years old at the time, and both her past and future bore down on her. Marriage or life in the convent were the only options available to any girl of her time, unleashing within her a conflict between the opposing forces of her nature. Although she had much respect for nuns, she was repulsed by the idea of becoming one herself. She was not opposed to the idea of marriage, but she was fearful of it. Existing in an anxious state of indecision for over a year, she asked the nuns to pray that God would guide her in her choice of vocation. She grew sick, and came to feel later that God was providing her with an opportunity for insight into what she should do with her life, for as a result of this illness she came to visit the home of her uncle. At his request, she read aloud to him from his devotional books, and over the course of a few days, her sense of vocation was born to her conscious mind. In her own words:

> *Though I stayed here for only a few days, such was the impression made on my heart by the words of God, both as read and as heard, and the excellence of my uncle's company, that I began to understand the truth, which I had learned as a child, that all things are nothing, and that the world is vanity and will soon pass away. I began to fear that, if I had died of my illness, I should have gone to hell; and though, even then, I could not incline my will to being a nun, I saw that this was the best and safest state, and so, little by little, I determined to force myself to embrace it.*
>
> *This conflict lasted for three months. I used to try to convince myself by using the following argument. The trials and distresses of being a nun could not be greater than those of purgatory and I had fully deserved to be in hell. It would not be a great matter to spend my life as though I were in purgatory if afterwards I were to go straight to Heaven, which was what I desired. This decision, then, to enter the religious life seems to have been inspired by servile fear more than love. . . . I had many temptations in those days.*

As an older woman, Teresa would read Augustine's *Confessions* and identify with him (along with all the

mortal saints and immortal callings

other sinful saints, she says). But whereas Augustine grappled with his transgressions as a mature man, a man capable of complex intellectual and emotional reasoning and confident of God's love, Teresa did so in the isolation chamber of her adolescence. The passions and fears of an eighteen-year-old can be overwhelming in the best of circumstances, and, with the Spanish Inquisition in full swing, the young Teresa wrestled with her anxieties of conscience during dangerous times. Whether her sin was grave or not, her desire to save herself from it was paramount, and determined her choice of vocation.

Many would doubtless propose that this turn of events was an example of the mysterious way in which God works, her remarkable life growing out of the "sinful" decisions she made as a teenager (sinful or not), impelling her to follow a path unappealing to her native inclinations at the time. I am inclined to agree, for I have known too many people in my life who have had difficult situations forced upon them, it would seem, only to later surface with a sense of profound gratitude for having had the opportunity to do something that they never, if left to their own volition, would have chosen. Thus Teresa's individual experience, though formed as it were by the specific time and place in which she lived, with its heavy emphasis on hell and damnation, speaks toward what seems an arche-typal truth we all share: that at times we must bring our will into conformity with circumstance, and in so doing find our true calling.

Teresa wanted to regain the grace of God by becoming a nun but did not want to entirely renounce the pleasures of the world. Toward this end, she entered the Carmelite Convent of the Incarnation as opposed to the Augustinian convent to which her father had sent her to board. The Augustinian nuns, she says, practiced their virtue in a way that seemed to her "altogether excessive," whereas the Carmelite nuns socialized in the parlor with both male and female guests, the well-to-do retaining the titles and privileges of their class.

Teresa, for her part, was granted her own sleeping quarters, kitchen, and private oratory. Friends and family would descend upon her, leaving behind gifts and very little time for sequestered prayer. Beset with distractions, she would try to pray but watched the hourglass instead. She suffered serious illness, lived in a semi-paralyzed state for three years, and generally thenceforth endured an uninspired religious life until the age of thirty-nine.

Spiritual awakening came just as her "soul was growing weary" and desired to rest. She began to sense "interior voices." Upon entering the oratory one day, she saw an image representing Christ sorely wounded. As in her youth when, while reading to her uncle, she was struck by the truths of her childhood, so the image in front of her unveiled itself with what was for her the penetrating reality that Christ had "suffered for us." Shamed by how little she had given Him in return, she threw herself at His feet, wept, and begged for the strength to not offend Him. She had by this point in her life lost all

mortal saints and immortal callings

trust in herself, she says, and placed therefore all her confidence in God.

In the nearly thirty years that followed, her well-documented life as mystic, writer, reformer, foundress of the Discalced Carmelites, and guide to the nuns under her care gradually unfolded. But though she wrote books on prayer and spiritual progress and fell into raptures, though Christ stood before her, "stern and grave," and showed her His hands, so beautiful no words could describe them, she would never seem in her heart to forget the initial impulse of her calling: The nuns gathered round her at her death tell us that her final words, spoken to God, were of a contrite heart and the hope that she'd been forgiven.

It seems as though we all find an element of archetypal truth in the magnificent life and writings of Teresa, or, more specifically, as regards the subject of this book, we may find here penetrating insights that help to move our own vocations forward. When still alive, she exerted much influence on such figures as John of the Cross, whose fate galvanized when at the formative age of twenty-five he met Teresa and in comradeship with her undertook a reform of the male branch of the Carmelite order. In the centuries that followed, she inspired innumerable brilliant creators—as diverse a grouping as Bernini, Henry Wadsworth Longfellow, and Carl Jung. Her writings provided spiritual nourishment to the young Carmelite nun Thérèse of Lisieux when the latter didn't find the guidance she desired from her elders in the convent. The Carmelite martyr and philosopher Edith Stein converted to Catholicism when she read Teresa's autobiography. In Teresa of Ávila, Dorothy Day, founder of the Catholic Worker in nineteen-thirties New York City, discovered a saint who understood our modern-day "weariness of soul," a visionary who could help to wrest us from the shadow of death, which for Day meant the sloth of effort we can allow ourselves to endure, year after year, until our lives are spent.

For myself, of all the things I learned from reading Teresa, one of the most relevant to my life at the time centered around her many discussions of the devil. I came to read *The Life of the Holy Mother Teresa of Jesus* at the age of thirty-eight, when for years I had been struggling with the big three internal cinderblocks of fear, judgment, and insecurity. Though I knew very well how destructive these unwieldy emotions could be, it never occurred to me to think of them as temptations of the devil—that is, not until reading Teresa's autobiography. Written at the behest of her confessors, uncertain as they were if her raptures and visions were of God or of the devil, Teresa allayed their suspicions and fears about her supernatural experiences, not by denying consort with the fallen archangel, but by assuring them that she had indeed come to know the devil well, and was thus most clearly able to ascertain those gifts that were God's own. In proving this to them, she records in discreet terms, and for posterity, her relation to both the dark side as well as the light—thus providing us with the means, to paraphrase Teresa, by which to recognize the devil's hand.

The most striking description to me was the evocation of his invisible presence within, descriptions I (and I suspect many other readers) recognized in my own experiences, moods, and behaviors: "I have seldom seen him in bodily form, but often, . . . although he took no form, I have clearly known he was there," she says. "His part in an experience can be detected by the restlessness and discomfort with which it begins, by the turmoil that he creates in the soul, . . . by the darkness and affliction into which he plunges it, and by its subsequent dryness and indisposition for prayer or anything else that is good. He seems to stifle the soul and constrict the body, making them both useless." She describes him as that interior presence, that nagging sensation, that prevents us from thinking a single good thought, interferes with our ability to concentrate and pray, destroys our sense of wholeness, robs us of pleasure, and sows doubts in our efforts and those of others.

To run her thoughts through the mill of contemporary metaphor, he sometimes took form as the all-too-familiar "internal critic." It was, after all, in this capacity that he visited her after she finally succeeded in founding Joseph's, her first reformed Carmelite convent in Ávila. Within three or four hours of its official opening, she reports, a voice within suggested to her that founding Joseph's might have been wrong. He asked her if she really thought "the sisters would be happy, living under so strict a rule, whether they might not go short of food, indeed whether the whole venture was not ridiculous. . . ." He asked her whether, being prone to illness as she was, she really thought she could live in so strict a house. Her descriptions of this profound moment go on at great length, and I would refer you to two wonderful translations, J. M. Cohen's and E. Allison Peers', to experience for yourself the thrill of recognizing, as did I, your own internal critic through the personal and moving details Teresa of Ávila divulges of her own conversation with the devil.

In her autobiography, we encounter a devil that we can recognize at work in our everyday life—not merely some suspicious, malevolent *other*, but a critic and judge inside our own minds, restlessly stirring about, tearing at people, places, and things, shredding the delicate fabric of our being. Through our own desire for honors, possessions, and pleasures, Teresa states, demons "join forces with us," leading us to feel suspicion, jealousy, uneasiness, apprehension, self-doubt, faithlessness, false humility, dryness, numbness, weariness, "each fragment [of the soul] seeming to go its own way."

Few days go by now that I don't sense the multifarious presence of this devil, though taking solace and strength in what I have come to find, as Teresa points out: that consciousness of his presence goes a long way toward vanquishing him; that God, in the end, permits the devil to "*stir*," such that we might learn more about ourselves, demanding that our inner beings "emerge from the crucible like gold," or perish. The eminent Carl Jung comes to mind and the presence of the "shadow"—the so-called "*nigrido*" at the heart of alchemical transmutation.

How to separate the dark from the light, and, more-over, to understand that without dark there is no light. Finding our own true center. Showing perspicacity in the people we choose to spend time with. The value of cheer-fulness. The importance of being fully what we are in the world. Holding ourselves in high esteem. Reconciling a mass of opposing characteristics. Accepting what we know in our hearts to be right though it impinges on our desire for freedom. Enduring a long gestation. Persistence in the pursuit of perfection. The clarifying potential of suffering. Losing trust that we alone can pursue our path and turning to God for help.

These and the many other treasures of Teresa's life come back, in my mind, to the moment when she sat with her uncle trying to figure out what to do with her life and the words she read sank into her heart. She tells us, you remember, that she suddenly recalled the truth of her childhood that she and one of her brothers had felt from a very young age: "It used to cause us great astonishment when we were told that both pain and glory would last for ever. We would spend long periods talking about this, and we liked to repeat again and again, "For ever-ever-ever!"

Oh that we were able to stand next to Teresa for a moment contemplating our journey ahead, that we could avail ourselves to God, our eyes closed, innocent of heart, eternity beyond the Castilian plain and everywhere else, all things vanity, weightless.

4
devotion

FRA ANGELICO

*Brother Giovanni Angelico of Fiesole (known in the world as
Guido) was no less an excellent painter and illuminator than
a worthy priest, and he deserves for both of these reasons to
be greatly honoured by posterity.*

GIORGIO VASARI

THE YEAR WAS 2002. I WAS STUDYING ART IN FLORENCE, Italy, where there was throughout the urban fabric a general devotional presence, a relationship between the hand and the mind, that drew forth from within me a deep nostalgia for a time and a place when beauty seemed a more inevitable product of human labor than it is today. Churches and street scapes were stacked and carved—a tapestry of craftsmanship layered century upon century, based upon the belief that the careful smithing, milling, and putting together of things mattered. In cloistered hallways and chambers scattered through the city were hung countless humbling and awe-inspiring works, including some of the most notable paintings and sculptures of Michelangelo, Leonardo da Vinci, and Fra Angelico, patron saint of artists.

Aside from the almost accidental way in which I encountered their work, biking purposefully to and from the academy each day, I knew that I merely skipped across the surface of a vast ocean whose depths were measured by the reach of faith. Within the north-lit studio where I stood from eight o'clock in the morning until nine o'clock at night, I stared into and only at the light falling on white plaster casts and nude models, completely immersed in what we were encouraged to consider to be the fundamental aspects of art-making: the pursuit of a practical course in the concrete understanding of how "to build a painting." My preoccupations centered around how to put charcoal on paper, how to assess the aspect ratio of an object, how to compare what I saw to what I drew, and how to create an accurate transposition of three-dimensional reality within a two-dimensional picture plane. Rarely did studio conversation stray from the analysis of height, width, lightness, darkness, and other verifiable parameters of visual phenomena.

I followed these discussions from the wide world of art I'd fallen in love with into the cramped quarters of ambition, measuring, as a friend remarked to me once, the long-term gain with a short-term yardstick.

Not more than a fifteen-minute walk away, Fra Angelico's most famous frescoes trembled on the surface of the walls at the Monastery of San Marco. Had I taken the effort to build into my days the ritual of spending time with his work, his images would have anchored me, would have reminded me of the importance of devotion—as opposed to diligence. Rather than walking across town, though, I remained in my studio, working hard to gain ground, losing all perspective.

Within any discipline, we must learn the language of our trade before we can take our place within it. Before writers can draft a story or essay they must master grammar and syntax; before doctors can care for a patient, they must understand anatomy, pathology, modalities of treatment. The Renaissance masters, from painters to engineers to architects, knew the business of their craft. Fra Angelico, in his time and to this day, was considered a supreme master of "technique." His paintings exhibit a rarely equaled fineness of execution and innovation.

But in an age of reason, pragmatism, and concrete analysis such as ours, there is the danger that technique, once a means to an end, becomes an end in itself. A danger that achievement, when assuming an *a priori* position in our lives, makes the very thing we strive for impossible to achieve. Fra Angelico provides for us an indication that in following a simplified pragmatic course, the grand possibilities of our trades may actually elude us.

Perhaps nowhere is it more obvious than in the frescoes on the walls of San Marco that the greatness of Renaissance achievement is grounded in spiritual and emotional depth, a "genius" that is obviously more than any single artist's ability to draw or paint with skill and precision. It is not skill in and of itself that made it possible for Fra Angelico to conceive of Christ mocked, blindfolded, surrounded by spiteful, disembodied hands. Technical prowess alone could never have led him to know that Mary, an adolescent girl, would feel self-conscious when visited by Gabriel, crossing her hands at her waist, bowing in submission. That is, unless we assume a definition unlike the one we use today for skill and technical prowess.

Hardly a trace of the history of Fra Angelico's life remains beyond his works. He left us no written record of his private thoughts, aspirations, or intentions. Our sparse biographical information is inferred from ledger entries concerning such matters as payments for commissioned works. Giorgio Vasari, his first biographer, devoted a chapter of his work *The Lives of the Artists* to Fra Angelico, but, published a hundred years after the artist died, it can be little more than inference and anecdote, presumedly lacking in factual detail. We don't know how many assistants Fra Angelico employed in his workshop or who they were. Of the paintings attributed to his work-shop, we don't know for certain which of them were by his hand and which were executed by his assistants. The names of his teachers have vanished from history. In general, a great aura of mystery surrounds his already mysterious works. Did his aspirations ever conflict with the spiritual imperatives of his mendicant order? Did the act of praying before he placed a brushstroke have influence on what we now see?

Though we're not sure of when or where he was born— sometime in the late 1390s, somewhere in Tuscany, the area of central Italy that gave birth to the Renaissance— we do know that by 1417 Fra Angelico (then known by his baptismal name of Guido de Piero) had moved to Florence with his brother to work in the manuscript industry, he as an illuminator, his brother as a scribe. In 1418, when still known as Piero, and not yet a friar, he painted one of his earliest known works—an altarpiece for the Gherandini chapel of the church of Santo Stefano al Ponte in Florence. Sometime between 1418 and 1423 he became a Dominican friar and took up residence at the poor and tiny monastery of San Domenico in Fiesole, a village on the outskirts of Florence. As a symbol of leaving the world behind, he took a new name, that of *Fra Giovanni da Fiesole*.

The Dominicans, a mendicant order founded in the thirteenth century by St. Dominic, offered to their friars a life synthesizing contemplation and apostolic ministry. "To contemplate and give to others the fruits of contemplation" was their credo. The hours of prayer, contemplation, study, and community service that would have comprised Fra Angelico's daily life invariably, by their very nature, left no evident trace. But through the commissions he undertook, always and only with the approval of his superiors, we perceive the blossoming inner depths of a man—paintings so beautiful that, to paraphrase Vasari, they can hardly be described, ever more luminous and more living with each passing year.

In 1429 he painted a triptych for the Camaldolese nuns in San Pietro Martire, the ten florins he was paid—a sum that went into the community coffer—recorded in the ledger of the San Domenico convent in Fiesole. The Virgin and Child are framed in gold, God the Father above, Sts. Dominic and John the Baptist, Sts. Peter Martyr and Thomas Aquinas to either side. Within the gold above the heads of the saints hover miniature medallions of the Annunciation—a theme Fra Angelico returned to over and again—while at the top of the painting scenes from the life of Peter Martyr unspool in the three pinnacles. In one he preaches to the masses; in another he writes in letters of his own blood the words *Credo deu R* as the executioner prepares to drop his blade. The dark and formal elements of the Gothic tradition from which Fra Angelico emerged as an artist are everywhere broken by rhymes of color, rhythm, and symmetry of mass, an interlacing of living detail that creates a quiet but forceful sense of new life breaking through—the great awakening of the Renaissance.

In 1428, Fra Angelico took gold, traditionally used in backgrounds, and drew into it the luminous figures of Christ and Mary in his *Virgin and Child Enthroned*. The *Last Judgment* he began in 1431 for the Camaldolese nuns of Santa Maria degli Angeli is a painting that inspires more of a yearning for paradise than any terror of hell: a centrally oriented and radiant Christ; the saved in harmonious symmetry to one side; the chaotic masses of the damned on the other. An enormous cemetery stretching to the horizon is all that remains of the world once John's final revelation has come to pass, yet it is the angels dancing in the garden, the joyful greetings of friends falling into one another's arms at the gates of paradise, that draw the eye.

In 1433, the full radiance of his vision began to shine in *The Linaiuoli Triptych* which he painted for the Linen Weavers' guild. Sts. Peter and Mark guard the outer doors of the triptych, which open to another of Fra Angelico's Madonnas. She is a treasure of molten gold and blue encircled by angels playing divine music while John the Baptist and John the Evangelist, respectively, stand witness on either side. With this piece, a man more deeply committed to his religious order than immersed in the artistic milieu of his time, broke out of the Gothic conventions he'd inherited as he delivered one of the first fully born images of the Renaissance.

In 1436 he painted the dead Christ stretched over the knees of mourners, their unprecedented individual faces full of life's gesture and emotion. In 1438 came the San Marco altarpiece, in which Fra Angelico first implemented the principle of perspective, codified by Leo Battista Alberti only a few years earlier. As the elements of the composition converge toward the vanishing point, Cosmas, a third-century martyr who practiced medicine without accepting a fee, turns to look at us, making eye contact with the viewer, directly communicating the intelligence of his compassion and conviction of purpose.

Fra Angelico moved his workshop from San Domenico to San Marco in 1440, and for five years he focused on the paintings referred to by Pope John Paul II as Fra Angelico's miracles. It is there he painted, in the cells of the monks, frescoes never meant for public eyes. His *Christ Mocked* and *Noli Me Tangere* were created for his peers in the convent who through contemplation hoped to draw closer to God. The latter painting shows Mary Magdalene reaching toward Christ and Christ seeming to reach toward her, though as the Gospel story relates, he would have been pushing her away. Their hands fail to meet, the atmosphere between them electric. Trees reach up toward the dawn-lit sky in a great wave of life, the bloody holes on Christ's hands and feet at one in color with the poppies that scatter the ground.

As Vasari tells us, "By means of these many works, Fra Angelico's fame spread throughout Italy." From his obscure origins, he was summoned to Rome by Pope Nicholas to undertake monumental fresco cycles in St. Peter's Basilica and the Vatican Palace. There he painted a *Deposition from the Cross*, scenes from the life of St. Laurence, an Annunciation, scenes from the life of Christ, and portraits of several prominent people of the time. When he returned for five years to Florence and San

mortal saints and immortal callings

Domenico of Fiesole before again being summoned to Rome in 1453, he had, by all accounts, ascended to the highest levels of his profession.

Yet Vasari tells us of a man who remained his entire life free of ambition, a man whose spirit, I feel, is evident in the very works that brought him such renown, though as I mentioned earlier, Vasari's biography is considered at best historical inference.

Fra Angelico cared nothing about that which concerned other people, says Vasari. He could have been rich, but because he believed that "true wealth was nothing but being content with little," he gave up a secular life of assured success to join a mendicant order. He was both an "excellent painter" and a "worthy priest": calm, gentle, and "inherently good." He subjugated his personal authority to a higher authority, turning to the prior for permission to eat meat or undertake a commission, turning to God for permission to paint. He befriended the poor, never lost his temper, smiled at the inadequacies of others, and neither felt capable of leading other people, nor wished to assume positions of power. When Pope Eugenius recognized Fra Angelico's "holy, quiet, modest" life and wanted to name him Archbishop of Florence, Fra Angelico suggested another man instead.

He applied himself to nothing but holy subjects and was unable to paint a crucifix without weeping. He prayed as he worked and never returned to a brushstroke after laying it down, believing the will of God was in every mark.

Concerned as we are these days with verifiability and historical truth, it is easy to dismiss Vasari's account as legend, the mythologizing of a man long dead. This skepticism, a natural condition of our practical time, sounds clearly in the tone and observations of William Hood, a contemporary art historian who writes about Fra Angelico and the Dominican Community of which he was a part. Compare Vasari's interpretation of Fra Angelico to that of Hood's.

> *Vasari: Although he could have lived most comfortably in the secular world, and in addition to what he already owned, could have earned whatever he wanted from the arts . . . he nevertheless desired, for his own satisfaction and tranquility . . . and, principally, for the salvation of his soul, to join the Order of the Preaching Friars. . . ."*

> *Hood: Nothing allows one to think that the young artisan became a friar for other than religious reasons. But there can also be no doubt that before long his new affiliation had perhaps unforeseen professional consequences. Fra Angelico profited from the patronage network to which the Order exposed him, a network that would likely never have been his had he remained in the lay state.*

It is not that Hood casts aspersions on Fra Angelico's motives as a friar or artist Hood has written a beautiful and well-studied book on San Marco, one I have on my own shelf and would recommend to others. But just as

Vasari speaks of him from the perspective of 1550, so Hood interprets Fra Angelico from the perspective of late-twentieth-century American culture and, in so doing, clouds in the reader's mind a life of devotion and vocation with that of profit and fame.

Hood continues, scratching at the roots of Fra Angelico's success by pointing out that Fra Angelico hadn't access to many of the things he would have seemed to need to achieve renown in fifteenth-century Florence. He hadn't been formally trained in the technical skills associated with large-scale painting and therefore had to teach himself; he didn't have family connections that would have helped him to launch a career; he had no famous teachers, mentors, and patrons; and, moreover, and most unbelievable, he implies, he had no personal ambition or un-attenuated time to focus. This list is not any different from the one I would make were I to describe what we must have in some proportion today if we are to achieve, to compete, within our chosen careers.

Hood asks: "To what, then, may we attribute his apparently unimpeded ascent to the highest levels of his profession?"

To this I would respond, "The difference between 'profession' and 'vocation.'"

Hood's answer, though, is "the very great talent" with which Fra Angelico was born, and his movement from commission to commission with the "instinctive and even predatory energy of a latent talent discovering its own potential. . . ."

This, indeed, is the answer our culture most readily gives to us. It is the answer I, too, would have instinctively gravitated toward were I asked how someone lacking all practical accoutrements of success could have nonetheless ascended to such heights of creative inspiration. It is hard for me to take the word "predatory" and apply it to anything I see or imagine when I experience a Fra Angelico painting, though. It is hard for me to believe that there was not some "Otherness" governing his way, an otherness that made it possible for him to achieve things that might otherwise have been beyond the scope of his power.

When I stood in the Monastery of San Marco, what I saw on those walls—what confronted me on the streets of Florence outside its walls—was skill rooted in vision, talent springing from love, technical excellence inseparable from non-commercial devotion, or so I believe. What confronted me was work beyond the capacity of ordinary endeavor. What confronted me was the inevitable question as to what talent truly is and the irrational, unsupportable feeling that Fra Angelico, Michelangelo, Leonardo da Vinci, Florence itself, and the craftsmen of all sorts over the centuries who made the city what it is today, rose from plague and corruption, rose from the constraints of average human endeavor, because the seemingly practical steps they took toward achievement were founded upon something greater than technical prowess and individual ambition.

5

becoming what one must

HILDEGARD OF BINGEN, MOTHER TERESA, AND SAINT AGNES

Remember that you have only one soul; that you have only one death to die; that you have only one life, which is short and has to be lived by you alone; and that there is only one glory, which is eternal. If you do this, there will be many things about which you care nothing.

ST. TERESA OF ÁVILA

AT TIMES WE ALL SEEM TO HAVE AN INSTINCT TO FOLLOW IN the path of others. As a child, I often looked to the characters in books as models, drawn to the women and girls who, like Joan of Arc, drew upon their strength and wit. I identified with figures such as Athena, with Laura in *Little House on the Prairie*, with Jo in *Little Women*— women who forged their way into uncharted territory, places they might not have been thought to "belong."

Helen Keller, who saw, heard, and spoke more clearly than most though she lacked the physical bearings of her senses; Nancy Drew, who solved mysteries that others couldn't; Marie Curie, who perceived hidden things, the light penetrating the darkness of *corpus humanum*— these were some of the people I admired most, people with their own special connection to the miraculous.

In spite of my belief that I would follow in the path of these women, I went out into the world to find myself, as most of us do, increasingly influenced by the flesh-and-blood presence of my peers. Gradually, I turned my gaze from the imaginary and long-gone figures who guided me through childhood and began to compare myself to those around me, in all of the myriad ways we do.

It was not until May 2003, my third and last trimester of study at the Florence Academy of Art, that I realized we're meant at a certain point to find our own way in life; that we're all meant, to paraphrase John Paul II, out of both our gifts and our circumstances, to create the masterpieces we're each called to make of our individual lives. I had for a long time rebelled against the notion that circumstances should matter, or be taken into account when you consider your future. I thought you ought to push ahead, no matter what, following your unbracketed path through life.

But my feelings about this began to change when I came to a disappointing juncture that spring in Florence: Though I hoped to become a painter, I could no longer afford to continue my studies toward that goal. In spite of moving from the spacious room I rented not far from the city center to a closet-sized chamber in the basement of a disintegrating nineteenth-century house, the amount of money I would need each month to eke out a living in Florence was simply nowhere to be found. I would have to turn down my scholarship for the coming year and in the not-too-distant future return to life, and work, in the United States. At the age of thirty-eight, I had reached a pivotal moment. After years of denial, I began to accept that we cannot always will ourselves to *overcome* adversity.

For me, the financial aspect of life had presented ongoing challenges from the time I'd left home at eighteen, the sort of challenges that others may confront in the form of circumstances such as illness, or rejection, or family responsibilities. For whatever reason, most of the people I've known come to a moment such as this, a moment when they cannot see their way forward. Regardless of why we've come to such a place, questions emerge: questions for which there are no easy answers, questions that, while they might have prowled in the subconscious, rarely break into the light of day.

Being in Italy at the time, I was surrounded by images of the saints: surrounded by their relics, memories, and miracles, surrounded by the spiritual mystery of their suffering. And it was clear to me that at a moment such as the one I faced, when an individual comes up against limitations that cannot be overcome, the story and callings of the saints endure.

For all of the iron-like will that many of the saints exhibit in their lives, there is often, I came to see, a corresponding *surrender*, a giving in to circumstances, not in the form of acceptance, but as a willingness to engage the time and place and the conditions of their life. Living as we have for centuries within a patriarchal culture, a multifarious array of constraints are particularly evident in the lives of women and the paths traditionally open for them. In the women saints, we can see more clearly than in their male counterparts, fates shaped to some degree by external conditions and expectations. Even among the strongest of them, magnificent careers were launched upon the foundations of what was simply available to them, as opposed to what they wanted: Teresa of Ávila had but two options as a young woman, marriage or the convent, and as she herself states in no uncertain terms, neither appealed to her. Thérèse of Lisieux wanted to become a missionary priest, a post available only to men. Instead she became a contemplative nun.

These are but two of the many women who speak of the way in which their fates were either determined or shaped by the limitations imposed upon them by the environment. There are many others who tell us, that what we are able to become is conditioned, to some extent, by the world we're born into.

I came to understand this in thinking, as part of the general recollection of my path, of three saints who'd been of interest to me when I was in my twenties: Hildegard of Bingen, Mother Teresa, and Agnes.

American feminists "discovered" the rich and inspiring life of Hildegard of Bingen in the late 1980's. A botanist and healer, visionary and preacher, a Benedictine abbess and multi-talented artist who wrote, composed music, and painted, she has come to stand as a symbol of the creative potential of female spirituality. While she was never formally canonized by the Roman Catholic Church, the Benedictines, the Church of England, and the Episcopal Church in the United States celebrate her feast on September 17. Many people, men and women alike, have come to find in her a kindred spirit, which was certainly the case with me when I was introduced to her in college. Learning as I was about the patriarchal constructs of Western civilization, I gravitated toward Hildegard of Bingen as an example of a woman who had excelled in a world where there'd often been few opportunities for women.

Captivated by her mandala-like paintings long before I knew what a mandala was, listening to her music without knowing it was prayer, awed by her visions though unable to comprehend them, I was enchanted by what I saw as the unimpeded flow of creative energy in her life, a flow that appeared as natural and effortless as a river. Because I did not then have enough experience to know that women sometimes struggle to find and maintain their "voices," because I did not then know that that which starts out strong in a girl can dwindle into silence,

I did not then, as I do now, think to wonder why and how Hildegard had been able to speak so clearly. Nor did I realize when I was eighteen that the life for which we know her unfurled like a flower after she passed, as she herself wrote in a letter, "through youth and attained the maturity when perfect power is gained."

Though from early childhood she experienced preternatural powers—at four describing in minute and accurate detail the unborn calf inside of a cow—not until the age of forty did she begin to live the active life we now associate with her: recording her visions from God, giving sermons, addressing emperors and popes (sometimes with admonitions), and healing the sick with her spiritual and botanical knowledge.

It was in 1136, after becoming prioress of the Benedictine abbey at which she'd served as a nun for nearly twenty years, that the life we now celebrate began to unfold. Shortly after taking on her new, more authoritative position, she began to experience visions unlike any she had had before, visions of fire coming from the sky and filling her mind and chest, visions she perceived not with her physical eyes but with her inner eyes and ears. Her confessor directed her to write down her visions, and when they were handed off to the archbishop of Mainz—later Pope Eugenius III—for inspection, her public life and career began.

To all exterior appearances, Hildegard was a fabulously successful woman who fully realized her potential and, yet, in her letters, we can and do at times glimpse a woman conscious of having given up who she *could have been* to become what she *had to be*. In a missive to Bernard of Clairvaux, she confided her feelings of frustration when she tried to express the fullness of her visions, lamented her lack of instruction in the German language, and apologized that she had no education "of an external kind," explaining that she'd been taught only in the "interior" of her soul. Reading this, we can't help wondering if she was particularly struck with what she didn't know in relation to the eloquent and highly educated man to whom she wrote, a man who would be named a Doctor of the Church, a man to whom she appears, in that most human of ways, to have compared herself.

Centuries later, it's nearly impossible to imagine Mother Teresa of Calcutta, a Blessed, as doing anything other than ministering to the poorest of the poor in Calcutta, work that seems clearly to have been her "calling," work that I, like so many, deeply admired when I became aware of it. But she, too, as I would learn, arrived at the role for which we know her gradually, step-by-step, after many years of first doing what she *could* as opposed to what she wished. Born in 1910 in Skopje, of Albanian Catholics, Agnes Bojaxhiu, as she was known before she became Mother Teresa, felt consciously drawn to vocational life in the purest sense of the term—the life of a religious, that of a nun—from the early age of twelve. The particulars of her calling took shape during her adolescence, as she read reports in the *Catholic Missions* that infused her with a desire to serve the poor in India. In 1928, though, the year

Agnes made her decision to become a nun, opportunities for women to serve as missionaries in India were limited.

A religious order in Ireland, the Loreto Sisters, which ran a foundation and schools for upper-class girls in India, brought her the closest she would come to fulfilling her desires by offering her an opportunity to serve as a teacher and nun in India. After joining the order as a postulant at the age of eighteen and studying English at their abbey in Dublin, Agnes began a two-year postulancy in Darjeeling, a fashionable summer headquarters for the British. In 1931, she took her first vows, adopting the new name of Teresa in honor of St. Thérèse of Lisieux. Soon after taking her vows, she went to Calcutta to work as a teacher, and for the next nineteen years she lived the life of a semi-enclosed nun and educator of upper-class girls at an exclusive boarding school in a walled-off compound within the city.

All of this changed in the early 1940s when human suffering in the already-troubled city of Calcutta escalated under the presence of famine, war, and natural disaster. Under the conditions of the time, she felt compelled to overlook her strict rules of enclosure, and as early as 1941 she is reported to have begun visiting slums and hospitals. Then, when a bloody massacre broke out between Muslims and Hindus on the sixteenth of August 1946, she was forced to go outside the convent in search of food for the nuns and the three hundred girls in their charge. The scenes of carnage and obvious human need reminded her of her early dreams of serving the poor of India.

About a month afterward, traveling to Darjeeling by train, Sister Teresa heard God's voice calling to her— what she later termed was a "call within a call." His message was clear. She was to leave the convent to live among the poor. To exist as a nun on the streets of Calcutta, aiding lepers, prostitutes, abandoned children, the sick and the dying, seemed nearly impossible, and many people, both within the church and without, viewed her with skepticism and outright hostility when she first stepped out of the Loreto Sisters' compound and began her new life of ministry.

In my own life, by the time I graduated from college, I had left behind both Hildegard of Bingen and Mother Teresa. I didn't then know the more complete story of their lives and struggles, and the little that I did know of them seemed to have little pertinent connection to the challenges I faced as I segued into a new period in my life, trying to take my place in the world and make my dreams a reality. For nearly a decade, no saints had any relevance to me until I started work on a novel that I had titled *Agnes Is Burning*. In part, this title referred to the church of St. Agnes in New York, damaged by arson. But the title was also an unconscious play upon the martyrdom of Agnes, the young Roman virgin of the fourth century whose beauty and wealth attracted many suitors. As the story goes, Agnes refused the many young men who sought her hand in marriage, answering to them all, Butler writes in his *Lives of the Saints*, that she had "consecrated her virginity to a heavenly husband." As she lived in pagan times, she was sentenced to burn to death for her beliefs. Saved from dying in a fire by a miracle, she was eventually beheaded instead.

Mired in my novel, trying to understand my otherwise intuitive relationship to it, I looked to Agnes as its muse, a guide, only to find myself uneasy with what I then saw as an over-weaning attention to martyrdom and virginity. As Robert Ellsberg points out in his book *All Saints,* the core story of Agnes is not about the "opposition of sex and virginity," but about the "conflict between a young woman's power in Christ to define her own identity versus a patriarchal culture's claim to identify her in terms of her sexuality. . . . "Virgin" in this case is another way of saying "free woman." In thinking back on Agnes, I could see that she fascinated me because she refused to submit to the preordained construct that had been imposed upon her. Unable to perceive the strange beauty of her fate at that earlier time, though, the deeper metaphorical inter-dependence of sacrifice and purity, I left the novel in an unfinished state and moved on.

When these saints appeared to me independently of one another over the years, they reflected back to me parts of myself—perhaps an example of the mirror-like quality present in most great mystics and spiritual leaders. I'd been interested in Hildegard of Bingen because of my burgeoning desire to become a writer and painter, in Mother Teresa because of concerns I had about social justice, and in Agnes because of an intuitive urge in one of my earliest novels. When Hildegard was displaced in my life by the examples of more contemporary women artists, when Mother Teresa's motives were challenged by her critics, and when I failed to understand the core of Agnes's story, I turned away from them, seeking other guides.

But taking them together, and knowing more about them than I once had, I found that their lives began to take on a wonderfully discrete and independent existence. They were whole and utterly distinct individuals, flowers, each of them, blooming from the roots of who they were and out of the earth into which they'd been planted. There they were, all of them women, strong and independent, yet so different from one another, just as is true of our closest friends. And, indeed, it wasn't hard to think of them as friends, assembled together for the first time in the same way that our living, flesh-and-blood friends, known at disparate times and places, may come together on some special occasion.

Hildegard, Teresa, Agnes: Here we see three women from entirely different times, three entirely different natures, three entirely different fates. Hildegard referred to herself as a little feather upheld by the wind, and in my mind's eye, she was a capable fifty-year-old aunt-like figure, petite and trim, with preternatural intimations of the world we'd come to inhabit, passing down to us the powerful gifts of nature and prayer through her tireless efforts at expression. The visage of Mother Teresa, one of the most photographed women of the twentieth century, need not be imagined, wizened and brown as a nut, as she graced the covers of so many magazines and periodicals over her long life of devotion and service. And then there was the young and radiantly beautiful Agnes: shining out of the altarpieces of the Renaissance, confident and loving, totally unafraid, completely unconcerned about the perceived strangeness of her convictions at the time and in the place in which she lived.

Like the subtle juxtaposition of neutral complementary colors, a soft red next to a tender green, a yellow next to violet, so the very special quality of their complementary achievements stood out to me in beautiful harmonic vibration. They had become fully each their own person not by following one another or anyone else, for that matter, but by becoming as fully themselves as they could within the time and place they lived.

All three of these women were challenged to forge their identities in a world where a woman's options were more strictly limited than they are today, and in this sense, there was no direct correlation between what I faced in the spring of 2003 in Florence and what they'd faced, each of them, within the distinct context of their time. And, yet, in a general way, each faced exterior barriers to what they wished to do, barriers that none of them *overcame* through the stubbornness of will alone. Agnes accepted the consequences of attempting to step outside the lines of that which bounded her, and Mother Teresa returned to her initial calling after a long period spent in the kind of service more readily available to a woman of her time. And with Hildegard of Bingen, a letter she wrote to Pope Anastasius IV illustrates how she dealt with not having received that which she might have wanted—an education that would have given her the tools she needed to more succinctly express the content of her visions—when she tells him that she was someone who didn't allow herself to be cast down by what was lacking in her.

In essence, I came to find that these women stand together to speak toward the power of working within the constraints of our own time and place, of the beauty that can be made manifest by embracing not what we want to be, but what we must become. It was not that they submitted to fate, or to external forces, but that they stepped forth from a position of disadvantage or oppression and through strength of will, persistence, vision, and faith expressed their vocation through the substance of the matter at hand.

6
the prodigal journey

SAINT AUGUSTINE OF HIPPO

The line that is straightest offers most resistance.

LEONARDO DA VINCI

IN 1998 I TURNED TO AUGUSTINE'S *CONFESSIONS*, AND I well remember the months I sat in a windowless room in an office in midtown New York reading the story of his conversion.

It should have been no surprise that I turned when I did to Augustine, the saint so fully identified with the prodigal journey, having just returned to the United States from a long journey of my own. Nearly two years had passed since my then-husband, John, and I left for Romania's Valley Olt, searching for the time to write, only to discover in the darkness of a far-off winter valley that our marriage had been a mistake. After deciding to separate, John returned to the United States, and I took up residence on a Turkish peninsula. I didn't know that I'd be returning to New York a year and a half later feeling as ragged and humble as the prodigal son in Rembrandt's depiction, but then I hadn't known I was setting off on my own prodigal journey—perhaps none of us do.

Not far away from where I lived those days in Turkey was Ephesus—that sacred place visited by the Virgin Mary near the end of her life, the place where John died and was buried, the place where seven young noblemen, Christians, were buried alive in a cave, only to wake thirty years later when the stone was rolled away from its entry. Pine, herbs, and flowers scented the air. Days were punctuated by the bellowing call for prayer, birds scattering from minarets into the sky, out over the blue Mediterranean.

Isolated and lonely, I passed hours walking, thrilled to find what must have been the arch of an overgrown Byzantine church, abandoned by the Greeks who had once farmed the surrounding land and fished the sea. The tessellated abstractions of turquoise that decorated the walls of the many and varied crumbling churches were all that remained of vanished frescoes—so little that it was impossible to discern anything but a ghost of the images that had once graced their surfaces. Many of my most cherished activities occupied these days. I painted water-colors of the mountains, the distinctly Mediterranean horizon, and the abandoned churches. I wrote each morning, page after faithful page, even as my story disintegrated before me. I anchored my spirit in the small collection of books I had on hand, a disparate mix of literature and art that included Daniel DeFoe's writings, Rembrandt's etchings, and *The Golden Legend*.

By teaching English in exchange for food and housing, I was able to stretch what money I had as far as I could, but it eventually ran out, and I had no choice but to return to New York.

From small rural dwellings, dark skies, and quiet mornings, to the rush and bustle of Western civilization, in very short order I began working as a temp for an outplacement firm in midtown. A windowless office was my new roost, broken up into a maze of carpeted grey workstations—a satellite office set up to service the growing number of people left without work during the massive downsizings of the mid-1990s.

Every morning I would walk from where I lived in Queens across the 59th Street Bridge to the Lexington Avenue subway, board the train to Grand Central, and maneuver my way through crowds of commuters. Surely, I thought, the little office that awaited me was either a warning of the fate in store for me were I to continue my misguided path, or an indication that I had already been consigned to one of the ten circles of hell. And for what? As I'm sure those who have found themselves in similar situations can attest, during the nights when I couldn't sleep, the mornings when I was pushed along by crowds, and the days as I sat in my ergonomically designed chair, wrapped in the buzz of white noise, I tried to figure out where I'd gone wrong.

During that period of time I came upon the Oxford paperback edition of Augustine's *Confessions,* its cover adorned with a luminous illustration of *Augustine in the Region of Dissimilarity,* taken from a fifteenth-century manuscript in the Basilica San Lorenzo. Although the phrase *region of dissimilarity* brought up an abundance of poetic speculations, it was the image of Augustine himself that captivated me. Within a painted floral frame of lapis lazuli, raw umber, and *terre verte,* the distraught bishop sat on the ground, elbows resting on his knees, hands shielding his face, tears streaming down his cheeks. The ground on which he crouched was devoid of vegetation but for a hopeful path disappearing behind him into distant green fields and white sand desert. A grove of fig trees surrounded him, a symbol of sin, I knew, but also a necessary compositional element to an otherwise empty picture plane.

Certainly one of the wonderful things about an autobiography, especially one written in the form of a confession, is the realization that the patterns of our lives have eternally unfolded, our experience, to some degree, the same as everyone else's. There are times when this may seem a horrifying thought, especially in our most rebellious and individualistic frames of mind, but in times of exile and alienation from ourselves and when we are pursuing a greater spiritual calling, we can take solace in the reaffirmation that we are, all of us, part of the human continuum, part of the community that suffers and grows and lives to see another day and tell about it.

In his *Confessions*, Augustine displayed the great gift of being able to drill down to the common core of our experience. And while on the one hand what he unfolds is the well-known story of his conversion, passed down since the fourth century, on the other hand, through his writings, he penetrates to a deeper understanding of how and why we might need to find a way to return from where we've gotten ourselves. In presenting his story, he did not seem like the stern and forbidding man I had anticipated, nor a particularly judgmental one as I had somehow been led to believe. Perhaps he was a misogynist, as I've been told, but no less a passionate and loyal friend, a man filled with astute insights, a man who looked his weaknesses and missteps squarely in the eyes and understood well the pressures of the world and the difficulty of following a straight and narrow path.

As October passed into November and New York City began to twinkle and buzz for the holidays, I followed Augustine's observations, thoughts, and feelings. Though by all outward appearances I was going about my days as a dutiful worker-bee shuffling down the chilly urban streets, my inner being was fully immersed in the time in which Augustine had lived, now so long ago, though not so dissimilar from the present with its appetite for "empty public shows" and materialism, a world where peer pressure swings its mighty battle-ax and men spar with their gifts and talents to acquire wealth and prestige. Though the particulars of our lives were different—he a man, a highly successful lawyer and rhetorician in the

Roman Empire of the fourth century; I a woman beating my circuitous path within what was then late twentieth-century America—it was impossible not to recognize that the transcendental truths he found in the most seemingly inconsequential daily events are equally relevant and available to us today if we mine our lives for meaning in the way Augustine did.

I identified with him when he described his early childhood prayers, the course of his life being altered by the books he read, his feelings of astonishment that a friend should die while others lived. "Here I was already thirty and still mucking about in the same mire in a state of indecision," he shares. In spite of his successes, life was not settling well for him, when, in one passage, he speculates that so often our attempts to fill our hungers can leave us bereft, emptier than before we set out, and schisms develop within when we base our choice of career on a desire for money and prestige rather than love. It was as if Augustine had discovered the core thoughts, observations, and behaviors—the molecular structure of spiritual and emotional life—that underpin our very existence.

Like most of us do, I suspect, Augustine got swept up in the river of life, steering his course as best he could, only to discover that in fact his will, the rudder of his destiny, had taken him only farther from God, farther from his innermost self. In searching for answers and direction, trying to discern at what point his alienation from God took its nascent leap, his thoughts progress from his earliest childhood memories, through the sexual adventures and peer pressures of adolescence to his education and professional successes in Carthage. Though he confesses that he longed in a vague but passionate way for love, he searched still for an object upon which to bestow his affection. And rather than turn to God—which would, he felt, require too much of a sacrifice—he buried himself in what he called a "sacrilegious quest for knowledge," building his life around an acquisitive, material paradigm, taking a mistress at the age of seventeen or eighteen, and otherwise forging ahead through the compromises of his age.

An important interaction happened upon him one night. While en route to deliver a speech for the emperor, he and his friends came across a beggar walking down the street. Although it was still fairly early in the day, the man was already drunk and in good spirits, joking and laughing. Augustine, on the other hand, was heavy with stress and anxiety, bringing him to reflect how the strange weight of *ambition*, the onerous load of mortal achievement, impels us to drag along the "burdens of unhappiness" in the pursuit of "a carefree cheerfulness." The beggar, he realized, had already achieved, by begging, the very thing he, Augustine, sought through "painfully twisted and roundabout ways." He compared the beggar's worry-free state to his own paroxysms, sure that he would prefer to be "merry than racked with fear," but no less preferring to be himself than the beggar. Neither he nor the beggar possessed true "honor and joy," he thought, for both of them were seeking their happiness in the "illusory intoxications" of drink and glory, respectively.

It was hard for Augustine to consider walking away from his life of ambition, but the encounter with the beggar—not so different than that of facing a panhandler on the streets today—was the beginning, it seemed to me, of many other such events that, one upon the other, wore away his barriers of resistance to change. He began to grow closer to God and godliness, and to follow his calling: to renounce his worldly career and turn his great gifts as a writer and thinker to the contemplation of God. He no longer burned with a lust for "honor and money." His career began to seem nothing more than "a servitude" to him.

Eventually, through the guidance of the bishop of Milan (a man who had lived "a long life of saintly zeal") Augustine confronts himself, lets go of unwanted habits, and, after nearly a lifetime of struggle and suffering, comes to find reconciliation between God and himself.

As I sat in that seventh-floor office of the job placement center where I worked, reading Augustine's *Confessions*, unemployed bankers would come in to dutifully go about their tasks aimed at fulfilling their job search requirements—making phone calls, using the computers, reading job-source newspapers and journals. And though I was supposed to be assisting them with their administrative needs, seldom did anyone ask for my help. In hindsight, it seems they must have felt to some degree a sense of humiliation (as we all would) over having been fired, preferring, as it appeared they did, to sit alone at their spartan desks, speaking in a low voice into the phone, leaving me to my readings. One woman, talking on the phone to her sister, raised her voice in a strange tone of question and declaration: "So, I've made some bad decisions in my life!" she said.

"It was with my consent that I came to the place where I did not wish to be," Augustine writes. Looking around the room, aware that all of us had ended up in that place, I wondered who had the courage to say so, the courage to admit that we were lost, the wisdom to acknowledge our own culpability, and the fortitude to change our life in every conceivable way. This was Augustine's path, and, though rife with fault, he was offering to us the proof of the possibility for change.

Near the end of his autobiography he puts forth the speculation that we seem to take more pleasure in things that are found and recovered than things never lost; that through loss, we find gain; that through grief, we find joy. And so it is that in straying from the core of our life we express the mystery of a nature that delights in recovery. As in the words of the hymn *Amazing Grace*—"I once was lost . . . but now am found"—so it is that we become lost, to Augustine's mind, so that we might return, both in our vocational and personal paths, to a life more fully in tune with the moral imperatives of our innermost natures, sanctified by the fortitude of our natural instinct to follow our true vocation.

The map Augustine has drawn of his own journey, as it shadows the archetypal way, suggests both the power of self-examination, and the need to take responsibility for where we've ended up; that in searching for a core meaning to ourselves and our lives, all our experiences and desires help redeem the high cost of our prodigal journeys, those circuitous pathways and byways that fill us with the treasures necessary for self-transformation—those missteps that create the chasms and distances we yearn to bridge, awakening, in essence, our hidden nostalgia for God.

As winter passed into spring, that year I read Augustine's *Confessions*, a new life emerged for me, one that I could not help realizing did, indeed, spring far from the place of exile in which I had been.

7

the little way, the high mountain

SAINT THÉRÈSE OF LISIEUX

There is a fine old story about a student who came to a rabbi and said, "In the olden days there were men who saw the face of God. Why don't they anymore?" The rabbi replied, "Because nowadays no one can stoop so low." One must stoop a little in order to fetch water from the stream.

CARL JUNG

IN DECEMBER 2003, I TRAVELED TO LISIEUX, FRANCE, THREE hours by train from where I was living at the time, in search of the elusive Thérèse of Lisieux. I had planned to stay in Lisieux for a week. But the city had suffered almost total damage in World War II and was very different from what I imagined it would be: wide avenues and concrete buildings replaced the timbered houses and narrow medieval streets of Thérèse's lifetime—not what I had expected, at all. Like fleeting memories of a dream, fragmentary glimpses of the town's once poetic beauty were left standing here and there, but mostly Lisieux felt like a newly built summer resort, replete with hotels, restaurants, and cafes, shut tight until the pilgrims return en masse for the next summer. What I went there seeking—to lay hold of Thérèse of Lisieux to understand what she had done, continued to elude me.

The basilica built in her honor on a hill overlooking the valley, one of the largest churches of the twentieth century, seemed at odds with her message of the "Little Way." The Carmelite convent where she lived as a cloistered nun for the last nine years of her very short life did not allow visitors inside its walls. The wax diorama of her life wasn't open in the winter. I did not find much of her life there to commune with, as I had hoped, in spite of an abundance of literature about her on sidewalk stands, in spite of the postcards bearing her pretty image coloring the quiet streets.

Not only did I find Thérèse as elusive in her hometown as I did from my house in Les Cerqueux Sous Passavant, but also I even felt turned away from my search for her by a strange encounter with two young American men at breakfast my first morning there. The twenty-four-year-old sister of one had joined a Carmelite convent in upstate New York, and the men were traveling to Carmelite shrines over their Christmas break from school, trying to understand why the girl they thought they'd known had joined a radical order, choosing a cloister for the rest of her life, sending her long dark hair back to her mother in a box, now only speaking to her family through a grille.

She became a Carmelite nun even though she was beautiful, her brother said to me as we sat at the long communal table at the retreat house dining hall, empty but for the three of us. "All the guys were after her." He took a picture out of his wallet, her image looking back at me with long dark hair and smiling eyes, he and his friend warm and sharing until they discovered through something I asked about the convent that I wasn't Catholic, yet was planning to write a book on saints. "Do you really think you can do that?" one of them queried in such a way that it left no question as to what he thought. He certainly didn't think I could or should. The open faces of both men quickly closed, and they got up from the table, leaving me to finish breakfast alone, their unspoken judgment accompanying me throughout the day as I walked the lonely streets of Lisieux.

For a moment, just a fleeting moment, I thought I'd come upon a clue to Thérèse when I visited the cathedral, which was spared by American bombers even as they obliterated the surrounding town in their necessary invasion of Normandy at the end of the war. There I discovered the tomb of Pierre Cauchon in the chapel where Thérèse used to pray. Pierre Cauchon was the head judge at Joan of Arc's trial in the city of Rouen, the man who sentenced her to burn in the city's old marketplace square, only a hour by train from Lisieux. Joan of Arc had been one of Thérèse's favorite saints, but, as

Cauchon's tomb was discovered in the chapel long after Thérèse had died, she wouldn't have known she prayed in front of the remains of the man who had sent her hero to her death. There must be a connection here, I thought, a connection between Thérèse, Pierre Cauchon, Joan of Arc, and somehow—in a very distant way—to myself and what I was searching for. But what that connection was I couldn't imagine, and baffled, I walked the streets of Lisieux, an outsider.

I had pursued Thérèse of Lisieux since coming across her biography by a French writer, M. D. Poinsenet, in the house I was renting. Given that I was researching saints and had been paying attention to their presence in my life, I had every reason to think that finding the book, both the only religious book and the only French book in the house, was no accident. It must have belonged to the former French owners of the property and sat perched on a shelf, small and worn, nearly indiscernible, between the works of writers like Noam Chomsky and Umberto Eco and dozens of guidebooks on France.

But if Thérèse did appear to me for a reason, she also came veiled, within the pages of a four-hundred-page biography that I hadn't yet the fluency in French to fully digest.

Entering her name into one of the many search engines on the Internet, I found the same understated story over and over again: At an early age, Thérèse felt called to join the Carmelite convent in her hometown, and, showing the courage and will so common in those compelled to undertake some special work in life, implored Pope Leo XIII to approve of her entering this austere order at an earlier age than was normally allowed. Her wish was granted, not by the Pope's intervention but by decree of the Bishop of Bayeux, and in 1888, at the age of fifteen, she said good-bye to her father and the outside world forever, stepping inside the walls of the Carmel in Lisieux, France, where she was to die of tuberculosis nine years later. In the last two years of what was, as is generally acknowledged, an "unremarkable life," she wrote a spiritual autobiography at the behest of her superiors, and upon that posthumously published work her sainthood rests.

Aside from the certainty and determination she felt in the face of her calling, there was little kinship, as far as I could tell, between the two of us. Her choice to withdraw from the world at fifteen to live in a Carmelite convent with a group of women who were mostly older than she was, what I saw as her over-weaning desire to become a saint (could one really admit to striving for such a thing and not immediately be disqualified someone had asked me), her seemingly suicidal desire to die young—all these impulses were foreign to me. I had made the choice to live in the world she'd cloistered herself from and couldn't imagine leaving—or could I, a little voice said, reminding me of my varied travels to far-off places. I naturally gravitated toward the heroic and formidable presence of a figure like Joan of Arc—but then so did she, I remembered, Thérèse having been photographed in the guise of the fifteenth-century warrior saint, a role she played in a performance at her convent.

And so I sat down in a café and began reading her autobiography, which I had picked up a little earlier at a bookstore near the retreat house. At first, her soft-spoken abstractions seemed as alien to me as her life, but the more I read and pondered her existence, the more I appreciated the many and surprising similarities, not just between her and me but perhaps among us all.

The life she described living in the convent was not unlike what I had experienced the past few years in the small worlds within a world in which I lived. The details differed, of course, for she was living a religious life in a cloistered order and I an artistic one within two separate communities devoted to painting, but both my experience and the experience Thérèse described would suggest that one of the spiritual functions of a community is to inculcate growth—through what is often an uncomfortable confrontation between one's own self, others, and the communities we form in cooperation with one another. I experienced some of the same dynamics in relation to the like-minded artists around me as Thérèse described having existed amongst the nuns in the Carmel in Lisieux, France, in 1888: competition; the desire for acknowledgment; a disproportionate amount of power (not always exercised justly) wielded by the leaders of the community; young aspirants seeking guidance from elders; a lot of tedious daily work that you hope will open the door to greater things; and, of course, the seemingly ever-present and otherwise petty social interactions that emerge over time, even among the best of friends.

In placing myself amidst these art communities, working on a daily level next to others, I exposed, as Thérèse writes of herself having done, my deepest desires, limitations, and gifts to others, showing the best and worst sides of my nature. On the surface, my days had been uneventful, as had hers: drawing from morning until night, writing in the evenings—but the pressure I felt to perform well, to prove myself worthy of what I sought to attain, imbued the simple act of drawing with the meaning of a much deeper drama. I had daily contact with students and teachers, peers and judges, some of whom I liked and some I didn't. Sometimes interactions left me feeling small, even humiliated, not always capable of acting with the kind of generosity toward others that I would have wished, not always acting with the grace under pressure that I feel sometimes so close to but sometimes so far away from. I often fell short of where I might otherwise have wished to be. All of this, Thérèse describes, her simple words evoking the archetypal course we follow, each of us, in our vocations.

My experiences and insights within these communities led me to a place similar to the one Thérèse described when she asserted, "I am only a poor unfledged bird." She had left the world and entered a convent, hoping to reach the stature of figures like Joan of Arc and Teresa of

Ávila, only to realize as she grew in spiritual understanding that their achievements were far greater, and
thus farther from her, then she ever imagined. I went out
into the world at eighteen armed with my love of literature
and art, thinking I would soon write stories of the caliber
of those I loved, in my thirties thinking that I'd soon
draw and paint with beauty. But, instead, I began to see
how great the works I love really are and how small my
own efforts were in comparison. In relation to my most
revered mentors—Dostoevsky, Joyce, Melville, and
Chekhov, Rembrandt and Titian—I am a poor unfledged
bird, indeed; just as, in relation to her mentors, Thérèse
felt smaller than small.

My life's work was not unfolding exactly as I thought
it would, those many years past in my youth, when I
dreamed of grand tomes of literary prose and beautiful
paintings, just as hers fell short of what she'd imagined
when she'd dreamed of burning for the Church or going
into the wilds as a missionary priest.

At the point of realizing that my life had not unfolded
as I thought it would I had hovered for several months
since leaving The Florence Academy of Art—I was still
hovering as I sat in a café across the street from the
Gothic cathedral, one of the few edifices, along with the
Carmel, left standing in 1944. My life, not yet fully lived,
obviously, was poised in confusion at this impasse, an
impasse Thérèse of Lisieux reached, as well, before she
continued on. Was it possible she appeared to me to
suggest a way forward from where I was?

The day waned on, and I paused for a moment in my reading to enjoy the last glance of light on the stones of the cathedral, contemplating the milestones along one of the paths we follow, one after another, side by side, day by day, generation after generation: Grand dreams; youthful fervor and ego; entering worlds that are, at best, oblivious to what we hope to achieve; tested in small and big ways alike; faced with qualities in ourselves that we wish we could change. Becoming more human, more loving, on a par, eye to eye, with everyone else. Comparing ourselves to the greatest of souls who have preceded us.

I ordered another coffee, reading on. Thérèse treated the realization that she was not to be exactly what she wished, painful though it must have been, as just another milestone on the path to her fruition and subsequent immortality. Her disappointment made it possible, in fact, for her to achieve what she did, for it was only when she realized that she could never be like those she admired that she found her own unique voice and a message of particular importance to those of us who live today. Accepting that she was only a poor, little unfledged bird in relation to the saints and martyrs whose lives she had hoped to emulate when she joined the cloister, she came to the following insight: "I am not an eagle. . . . What shall I do? . . . Die of grief at being so helpless? . . . Oh no! I shan't let it trouble me. . . . I know that Jesus . . . would not inspire me with such desires unless He meant to fulfill them. "

She did not allow herself to feel any doubt in what she aspired to do, and looked ahead to find a way befitting someone of her nature and place in the world—that of a middle-class girl in nineteenth-century France, who had assimilated and lived within the confines of Victorian society—to achieve something meaningful, even grand, within the container of the sheltered life she led. Her aspirations of sainthood undeniably high, the inclination of the path steep, steeper than she'd expected, she built what she called a "lift to heaven," or, "the Little Way of Spiritual Childhood," as she titled it, the doctrine for which she now is so well known. "We are loved not *in spite of* our smallness and faults but *because* of them," she said. As children endear themselves to their parents, so our "foolishness" endears us to God. At the dawn of a century of unmatched violence and destruction, she made a plea that we might love our neighbors and grant them charity—not the neighbor one already likes, but those who rake and scratch, if even ever so slightly, at one's sense of generosity.

"The most trivial work, the least action" she said, "when inspired by love, is often of greater merit than the most outstanding achievement."

This quiet, unheralded message lay fallow in her time, but within a century Thérèse was heralded as one of the great revolutionaries and "thinkers" of the Catholic Church, granted a position as "Doctor of the Church" for the simple and profound feeling of God's love that she had stooped to pick up from where it lay, almost forgotten, beneath us. She who died in obscurity, plagued in the last months of her life by spiritual darkness, was now a saint, guide, and co-patroness of France.

For myself, I was just surfacing from many years on the road, searching, the life of a veritable vagabond as second nature as waking in the morning. I lost my way at times, got tangled in the underbrush. Coming out of the dense thicket behind me I saw that instead of having arrived at a resting place, I had merely reached that point along the way where the trail begins to ascend.

I was glad I'd come to know Thérèse. She arrived at this point, too, and instead of giving up, she sat down for a moment to rest, looked around and left a message for those to come: "Trust that you are meant to do what you feel called to do. . . . [P]ay no attention to maps made by other people. . . . [Y]ou grew stronger on the first part of the journey, know yourself better, and have a clearer sense of where you are headed. . . . [N]ow let go of all of your expectations. Find a way forward. There is another milestone waiting." She left the message that we are to flap our "tiny wings," knowing that "all the eagles of heaven" will pity, protect, and defend us. She left the message that we ought not to hide our smallness but make it part of our project.

Systole, diastole. The heart contracts and expands. Ambition and achievement swell within the great arc of history, generations of inspired and inspiring effort, but we must shrink back sometimes before setting out, in order to remember the core of ourselves and acknowledge the little way.

8

grace

SAINTS BERNADETTE SOUBIROUS AND
EDITH STEIN

*I was able to sever the seemingly strongest ties with minimal
effort and fly away like a bird escaped from a snare.*

ST. EDITH STEIN

BERNADETTE SOUBIROUS AND EDITH STEIN WERE SISTERS, TO my mind, though outwardly they could not have been more unalike: the former an uneducated French girl of Basque origin, her childhood a tapestry of labor and subsistence living, hidden deep within the mid-nineteenth-century confines of a small town in the Pyrenees Mountains; the latter, an intellectual giant even in her youth, raised by a bourgeois Jewish family in early twentieth-century Germany to believe she could become whatever she wished.

With their portraits side by side in comparison, Edith gazed through deep brown-black, almond-shaped eyes with an unnervingly forthright seriousness, her hair slicked back, pulled tightly behind her head; Bernadette, so strikingly open and wordless, a Raphael portrait of youth, a mysterious pool of light, inviting the onlooker's gaze. In contemplating their vastly different figures, for quite some time I was vexed by my feelings of verisimilitude, sensing that between the two lay evidence to support my continued belief that we all share some degree of common experience, in spite of the many and varied paths that unfold before us.

What I have come to feel, regarding Edith Stein and Bernadette of Lourdes specifically, is that this shared experience has something to do with the presence of *grace*, a word I've never truly understood, a multifaceted, mercurial term that theologians have classified and defined over and again, filling hefty tomes in the wake of their efforts. We need only turn to the *Catholic Encyclopedia* for an example of the complexities inherent in defining that which seems to defy all definition.

For myself, I have tried in simplest terms to understand grace through metaphor. The feeling I have, for example, in reading about encounters with grace, as well as my own experiences, evoke the image of walking by a closed door whose latch suddenly releases, leaving it ajar with a thin sliver of vertical light between the edge and the jamb, illuminating an otherwise shadowed place. In taking the metaphor further, I have contemplated that, while grace may be the unlatched door and the glimpse of light, the question remains for us as to whether we walk by (though perhaps pausing first) or whether we open the door and walk through. This, it seems, is one of the moments of decision wherein our vocations take form; that is, one of the moments of decision wherein our lives either transform, or evolve away from, the habits that steer us toward an otherwise preconceived destiny.

It is not unusual to hear of people whose lives suddenly take on a new direction. On pilgrimage to Santiago de Compostela in the fall of 2004, I met a French real estate developer who decided to become a monk. A friend who was an architect received a fellowship to work in Rome for a year and left his career to become a painter upon seeing Caravaggio's paintings of Sts. Peter and Paul in Rome's Santa Maria del Popolo. Another friend, a poet, became a doctor in his early forties after a life-changing friendship with a heart surgeon. For myself, I have experienced moments where I seem to be invited to altogether re-imagine my life. Deciding to become a painter was one of few times I've acted upon such an invitation. Yet I've moved tentatively to open the door through which I saw a crack of light, fraught with self-doubt, hesitant to let go of what I imagined myself to be.

In Bernadette and Edith Stein, on the other hand, we find two women to whom the unveiling of purpose seemed as effortless and simple as the opening of a door and walking through.

Let us first return to the early years of Bernadette's life. To better understand why it unfolded as it did, it is important that we recognize the strained, and perhaps all-too-common, circumstances under which she developed in her formative years. Born in the small mountain town of Lourdes, she was the oldest of four children whose parents' alcoholism rendered them incapable of providing for their children's welfare. Until Bernadette was ten, she and her family lived in a large and rambling mill that they owned and operated on the outskirts of town. Even in this bucolic, country setting, unrestrained by the din of urban activity, her family plunged from one crisis to another. Under the burden of financial hardship, Bernadette had to forego schooling, her days consumed by household chores and the necessity of assuming responsibility for the care of her younger siblings.

The already modest estate that her family subsisted off of plummeted from bad to worse. Forced to relinquish their property to creditors—and in so doing, to surrender their respectable trade as millers—her parents began working as itinerant day laborers, moving from one temporary shelter to another, struggling to make ends meet. It was under these circumstances, in her early teens, that Bernadette experienced the first intimations of a life that was to be very different from the one that all other circumstances might have indicated to be her fate.

Thirteen, I have come to find, is a particularly potent age in the lives of female saints. It was the age Joan of Arc heard St. Michael in the garden, and the age Thérèse of Lisieux experienced what she called a "complete conversion," recovering the "strength of soul" she had lost when at the age of four her mother died. And it was the age when Teresa of Ávila implored the Virgin to take care of her in the wake of her own mother's death. For Bernadette, thirteen was the age "the Lady" appeared to her.

It was February, a cold time of year in the Pyrenees, and Bernadette had been given the task of going out to a nearby forest with her sister and a friend to collect firewood to cook and heat their home. While taking off her shoes and stockings at a small grotto, in preparation to cross a river, she heard a noise, "as if there was a rush of wind." She looked around; the trees and fields were still. She heard the noise again, looking toward the grotto, at which point she noticed "The Lady"—a woman dressed in white, calling to her, signaling for her to approach.

For Edith life was very different. At the age of thirteen, when Bernadette was wandering the wooded Pyrenees, Edith Stein, a generation later, sat in an apartment in Breslau, Germany, reading Shakespeare, whom she called her "daily bread." She was born to a devout Jewish family in 1891, with parents who were as responsible as Bernadette's were reckless. Her mother, an industrious and hardworking woman, took over the family lumber business after the death of her husband when Edith was two, taking her place with sure competence in a traditionally male trade.

As Edith describes in her autobiography, *Life in a Jewish Family*, books, education, music, language, and art filled her young years, as did the ever-loving presence of her mother, a reliable pillar of wisdom and strength.

mortal saints and immortal callings

Edith lived only for her studies, she writes, and the aspirations they awakened in her. "Smart Edith," her family called her, accusing her of being ambitious—and justly so, she says, for in her dreams she always foresaw a "brilliant future" for herself.

Whereas Bernadette referred to herself as a "nothing," an "ox," a "broom," Edith "dreamed about happiness and fame," convinced that she was destined for something great and did not belong "in the narrow bourgeois circumstances" into which she had been born. While Bernadette displayed a submissiveness in her relationship to her life and the specifics of her calling, Edith forged headlong in the face of family pressure to do exactly as she wished, driven by a sense of "inner necessity." Through Edith's autobiography, we can discern her tenaciousness and self-motivation, which at the time was directed at studying philosophy in spite of the pressures of her family to pursue a more practical course. Building upon her formidable intellectual talents, she received a doctoral degree in philosophy in 1916, firmly committed to what she then considered her destiny.

Though possessing a vast feeling for the spiritual, Edith guided her life, it seems to me, through her intellect. Even at a very young age, she expressed the tenor of an ethos that would continue to guide her path: "We are in the world to serve humanity. . . . We can best do so when doing that for which we have the requisite talents." Perhaps no better definition can be so succinctly applied to vocation.

Bernadette, whether through lack of education or because of her innate disposition, had little relationship to the thinking world; hers was instead a world of feeling and sensation, as exemplified in her first encounter with "the Lady," where, upon hearing the rushing sound of wind, she immediately turned to notice that the trees were still and knelt in prayer, full of unquestioning faith. In contrast, Edith seemed to have questioned all that she experienced, losing her faith, only to rediscover it over time. As a very young child, she recognized within herself a "hidden world," relating that whatever she saw or heard throughout her days was pondered there, but by the age of fifteen, she consciously stopped praying and declared herself an atheist. At twenty-one, she suffered a severe depression related to the meaning of life. In 1914, when she was twenty-three, she served as a Red Cross nurse in a hospital for wounded soldiers and in her own words was confronted by "the meaning of death, humanly speaking."

These confrontations with spiritual matters came to the fore of her conscious mind in 1917 when, in visiting a cathedral with a friend, she experienced her first definitive encounter with grace, as it pertains to our discussion of vocation.[1] As Edith and her friend contemplated the interior of the church, she noticed a woman enter with a basket under her arm and kneel for a short time in prayer. Struck by this, she was later to write, "Here, in the midst of daily affairs, someone came into an empty church as for a confidential exchange. I have never forgotten that."

mortal saints and immortal callings

Study and work eclipsed the years up to 1921 when she encountered another completely unforeseen and unsought moment of grace that perhaps best illustrates the idea of the sliver of light in an open doorway. She was staying in the house of a friend during a vacation and found herself alone one day. Her hostess invited her to make use of the library while she was away. In her own words, Edith describes the following: "I took at random a large book with the title *The Life of Saint Térèsa of Jesus, written by herself*. I began to read and I was immediately caught up in it and could not stop until I reached the end. When I closed the book, I said to myself: *There is the truth*."

Grace comes and goes quickly, a fleeting glimpse of light, an opportunity for change, a recognition of truth or of the sublime that moves us to stop and reconsider ourselves and the world. In Bernadette, we see a girl of thirteen gathering wood for her mother, looking over to a numinous apparition who graced her life for two weeks and never appeared to her again; in Edith Stein, we see a young philosopher stepping into a cathedral to witness a woman praying, and later having a chance encounter with a volume of writings. Both the grand and the commonplace, each with the power to transform, swept these women out of their local milieus, Bernadette to discover, Edith to clarify, vocations neither of them anticipated or sought.

After their visions, neither Bernadette's nor Edith's lives would ever be the same. On the spot where Bernadette had dug in the mud during one of the appearances of Mary, a spring appeared. In a short period of time, news of miracles had spread, and Lourdes became a major pilgrimage site.

Bernadette continued to live with her family, but, as both the town and the Catholic Church became aware of the implications of what had happened, church and state authorities invested themselves in Bernadette's fate. As the beneficiary of an extraordinary grace, officials felt, Bernadette's life ought to conform to an ideal of sanctity, whereas this was not the case as long as she lived with her disreputable family. They intervened in her life, and, relieved of household responsibilities, she began to attend a free public school, where, considered "backward," she learned to read and write only with difficulty. With the help of officials, her father was given the opportunity to run another mill, and the Soubirous family returned to a life not unlike the one Bernadette had known in her earliest childhood.

She, meanwhile, was separated from her family and began lodging at a municipal hospice run by a congregation of nuns known as the Sisters of Nevers.

Admitted as a "penniless invalid," she existed in a state of limbo for six years. She studied at the private school run by the sisters for the daughters of the well-to-do, battled life-threatening illness, and participated in the dog-and-pony show that had been forced upon her almost as soon as she'd seen the apparition at the grotto. Clerics, pilgrims, and the curious visited her, interrogated her, touched her, tore pieces of cloth from the clothes she wore, and requested gifts and prayers of her. Photographers took pictures of her praying in front of statues of the Virgin Mary, kneeling in front of the grotto, and holding the hand of the Superior of the hospice in Lourdes, portraits sold to help fund the financing of sanctuaries.

Yet, slowly during these difficult six years, Bernadette, who had once said that she could not imagine becoming anything, realized she had a special aptitude for caring for children and nursing the sick. In 1866, she joined the Sisters of Notre Dame of Nevers, where she spent the rest of her life as Sister Maria Bernarda. Not only would she have been unable to conceive of such a path before having experienced the apparitions, but, also, as an asthmatic, uneducated girl, one who lacked a dowry, she would ordinarily never have gained entrance to the convent as a nun.

After Edith Stein's conversion and subsequent baptism, her long-standing vocation as philosopher and educator took on a new dimension. She wanted to join the Carmelite order as a nun, but her spiritual advisors counseled her to remain in the world instead—at least in part out of consideration to her mother, whose sorrow at her daughter's conversion would have been even greater had Edith also encloistered herself. As a layperson, Edith taught German at a teacher's training college and girls' lyceum run by the Dominicans for a decade before being appointed lecturer at an Institute for Pedagogy. During these years, she continued to write (on, among other things, the vocation of women) and became a prominent leader of the Association of Catholic Women Teachers.

In 1933, forced to relinquish her position due to the rising tide of anti-Semitism in Germany, she entered the Carmelite Convent in Cologne, taking the name Teresa Benedicta of the Cross.

Bernadette and Edith are not alone in experiencing a dramatic change in their life and calling in the wake of grace. In any saint I might think of, we can find a vocational path clarified, unveiled, evolved, or changed through moments of grace, both sacred and profane: an encounter with a beggar on the street, the reading of a book, an act of kindness, a confession, the sunlight falling on the leaf of an orange tree, friendship, a dream, a vision, illness, the witnessing of injustice, the death of a friend, the contemplation of beauty, the space in between. To paraphrase the twentieth-century German-born theologian Paul Tillich, grace is that moment when the divine appears to inspire new being, to bring our essence in line with our existence, through nature, art, and religion.

We all have experienced such moments and felt them to be something special: a near-death experience in a car accident, inspiring us to live more in concert with our core values; eye contact with a homeless person, precip-itating actions that have lain dormant for years; the sight of a single tree on a vast plain, compelling us to tread more lightly as we go about our days; candles flickering in the twilight depths of a chapel, bringing silence.

Grace is a gift within the mortal condition we all share, a moment wherein the living essence of the divine is revealed, a moment wherein the patterns of the universe break through cloud cover in a fleeting display of brilliance and beauty, affirming to us how little of this great mystery we know or understand, perhaps inviting us to altogether reconsider how we live our lives, what we do, and why, perhaps offering us an entirely new path.

9
passing through youth

SAINT IGNATIUS LOYOLA AND
THE OTHER MATURE SAINTS

> *Age is not all decay; it is the ripening, the swelling, of the*
> *fresh life within, that withers and bursts the husks.*
>
> GEORGE MacDONALD

LIVING WELL WITHIN ONESELF, LIVING AT PEACE WITH A sense of accomplishment, is a formidable task in a world such as ours, where the obsession with youth denies us a graceful flowing into our middle and twilight years. While few careers we might think of are truly dependent on the strength and impulse of youth, there is nonetheless the inevitable celebration of prodigal talent even in professions that clearly benefit from maturity. I have become increasingly aware of this of late, as I transition into my forties, still evolving in my own sense of vocation. It is with a sense of relief when I do, on occasion, read of late bloomers, taking solace most recently in realizing that many of our most revered saints—all of whom were once living, breathing, sentient flesh—did not come into their own until having passed, as Hildegard of Bingen expresses, through the gauntlet of youth to attain the maturity when perfect power is gained.

For every St. Agnes or St. Foy, who flung themselves into the world with the passion and conviction only a child can sustain, there exists those who mature slowly. While the child martyrs, with their fresh enthusiasm and radiant beauty, remain inspiring witnesses to a long lineage of faith, those who come into their own later in life offer depth, perception, wisdom, patience, the judicious use of power—qualities that surface through trial and error, success and failure, and a continued immersion on the mortal plateau of cause and effect.

Ignatius Loyola, who founded what is best known today as the Jesuit order in the mid-sixteenth century, stands out prominently among these figures for me, for he became a student relatively late in life, consciously frustrated by the slow path he followed to the fulfillment of his aims. His life, though long and complex, can be summed up as that of a relatively frivolous and unquestioning youth who later went on to impact the course of history. Up to the age of thirty he had lived the life of a soldier when, in a battle against the French in Pamplona, Spain, he sustained serious injury to his legs. During his convalescence, he began reading books on the life of

Christ and lives of the saints, through which he experienced a slow conversion. When he was well enough, he spent three years traveling as a pilgrim, living as a beggar, and repenting the life he had lived, ushering in the beginning of a life very different from the one he had left.

As he began to realize that he wished to be of spiritual aid to others, an evolution of events would eventually lead him to become a priest. The first step on this path was his pursuit of further education, and he returned to Spain from the Holy Land to which he'd gone as a pilgrim, now in his early thirties, to begin studies in Latin, theology, and the humanities. Struggles and conflict with the Inquisition compelled him to set off for Paris, where he resumed his studies. Older than his fellow students at the university by many years, grappling with Latin at the age of thirty-seven in company with boys age nine and ten, he struggled to stay focused on completing his education when he felt already spiritually prepared to, as he said, "save souls." He was forty-three when he received his Master of Arts in 1534, an age, as one of his biographers points out, that must have seemed older in the sixteenth century than it seems today.

At forty-five, he was not yet a priest, though he'd begun to attract many followers to the order that grew up around him, the Society of Jesus, or the Jesuits, officially recognized by the pope in 1540 when Ignatius Loyola was forty-nine. He was by then nearly thirty years older than either St. Francis or St. Dominic when they started their respective orders.

mortal saints and immortal callings

Ignatius Loyola was not the only saint to slowly develop a full sense of purpose and the skills required to practice his vocation. Mother Teresa heard the call of God at twelve and left home at eighteen to become a nun, but it was not until she was thirty-eight that the conditions of the world in which she lived compelled her to leave her position as a teacher at St. Mary's High School in Calcutta to work with the poorest of the poor in the slums of the city. She was forty when she received permission from the Holy See to start her own order, "The Missionaries of Charity," beginning the labor for which she is now so well known. Hildegard of Bingen was also forty when she became the public figure we know her to be. And Teresa of Ávila, when in her mid-thirties, began a new chapter in her spiritual life, having undergone a conversion while praying before "Christ hanging poor and naked upon the Cross." By the time she composed her autobiography and established a reformed Carmelite convent in Ávila, she was forty seven.

Vincent de Paul was ordained a priest at the age of nineteen, yet the early years of his vocation were motivated not so much by the urge to help others as by the desire to escape the peasant class into which he'd been born. His devotion that earned him the title "Apostle for the poor" seems to have been emerged around 1617, when, at the age of thirty-six, he organized the first group of women, known as "Servants of the Poor," to help care for the less fortunate in his parish at Châtillon-les-Dombes. Though much of what transpired in his life before that point lay in shadows, we know that he disappeared at about the age of twenty-four—imprisoned, some speculate, after being accused of theft, though a letter by his own hand tells the riveting story, dismissed as legendary by many scholars, of having been captured and held as a slave in Tunisia.

If Vincent de Paul's narrative of being enslaved was fabricated, it suggests he felt ashamed of and thus had to mask the errant years of his youth. But it's impossible for me not to feel that his compassion for the prostitutes, prisoners, and destitute who lived in the shadows was watered through his years of slow maturation and growth—if not in a literal place of imprisonment, then in the darkness of his own inner self.

His colleague Louise de Marillac discovered her purpose in life in her late thirties upon meeting and developing a friendship with Vincent de Paul and subsequently co-founding with him the Daughters of Charity. Much of her life before then was wrapped in her regrets about the past—most specifically, that when she'd come of age, she'd not been given leave to become a nun as she desired but acquiesced instead to an arranged marriage, thus missing her calling, as she saw it, by many years.

The river of time—we see it as breaking us down and in many ways it does. It wears at our bodies, but it also flows back into the depths of our consciousness, nutrifying the soil in which we labor, turning it under, richer, deeper. We can never know if Louise would have known how to mother the Daughters of Charity had she herself not borne a child. We can never know if Ignatius Loyola would have started the Jesuit Order, sending out his "Soldiers of Christ," had he not experienced firsthand the sufferings of battle. But examples such as these provide evidence that early experiences in our lives inform later, seemingly unrelated endeavors, and that this maturation of our mortal selves is often a vital factor in the full realization of our vocational callings. Through such long and winding paths creative potential is realized, orders are founded, social progress forwarded, friendships deepened, and teachers and guides made available to those who will follow.

In my own mind, I keep a list of the saints whose purpose and ability bloomed as they progressed through life. In addition to the ones I've mentioned above, others I might mention include the following:

St. Bartolomé de las Casas: This Spanish priest who owned a plantation in Cuba run by indentured laborers, at the age of twenty-eight witnessed a massacre of Indians. Soon thereafter, he joined the Dominican order as a friar and spent the next fifty years of his life striving to expose and rectify the cruelties of the Spanish Conquest of the new world.

St. Augustine of Hippo: At the age of thirty-two he converted to Catholicism, renounced his former life of ambition, and became a monk.

St. Rita of Cascia: At the age of thirty-six, she joined the Augustinian convent near her home after many years spent trying to do so.

Angela of Foligno: At the age of thirty-seven, upon hearing a sermon, she left her wealthy and frivolous life to subsist on alms.

St. Alphonsus Rodriguez: At the age of forty-two, after having run a family business and been a husband and father, he made his final vows to the Society of Jesus and spent the next forty years of his life as a hall porter at the Jesuit College in Majorca.

Oscar de Romero, Archbishop of San Salvador: At the age of sixty, upon the assassination of a friend, he became an outspoken proponent of human rights after a timid career as a priest (an act that led to his own assassination in 1980).

A composite picture of youth based upon these saints suggests that, if it seems to us that we've missed an early flowering, we would do well to embrace age as that which liberates us from a youth that, while strong and free, can also be chains that bind. I'm sure that all of us can identify with the weaknesses that one saint after another reveals having needed to overcome—the follies of their youth. Teresa of Ávila, for example, tells us of her extreme vanity as a young woman and her preoccupation with gaining the admiration of others; Augustine speaks of having ambition to such a degree that he cast away the woman he loved to further his career; Charles de Foucauld writes of a reckless confidence that propagated a spiritually paralyzing degree of sloth. Ignatius Loyola could not imagine any other life than that for which he was raised, that of a soldier and an aristocrat.

A false sense of responsibility to fulfill the expectations of others, including family and society; inexperience that breeds insensitivity, impatience, and an inability to empathize; the wounds and baggage of childhood that impede spiritual growth; a paucity of self-knowledge that interferes with our ability to grasp the potential of our lives—these qualities, too, the saints demonstrate having had to outgrow.

Many saints tell us we are pilgrims in this world, and when I feel mournful over my vanishing youth, I think of what it might mean to be a pilgrim and again of Loyola, the pilgrim saint, forever walking from one place to another. Loyola set out from Spain to the Holy Land after his conversion and spent the rest of his life on a journey, embracing, it seems to me, that there is no pinnacle of achievement to be reached and that the efforts of our vocations are not a race to the top but a walk toward the sacred.

10
hidden life

CHARLES DE FOUCAULD

*Jesus came to Nazareth, the place of the hidden life, of
ordinary life, of family life, of prayer, work, obscurity,
silent virtues, practiced with no witnesses other than God,
his friends and neighbors. Nazareth, the place where
most people lead their lives.*

CHARLES DE FOUCAULD

IT WAS AFTER A FRENZIED SUNDAY MORNING IN NEW YORK
City, searching for the dessert I was to bring for an
upcoming dinner with the Little Brothers of the Gospel,
that I wandered down a busy street in the Bushwick sec-
tion of Brooklyn, one of those neighborhoods where
trees are scarce, homes are clad in aging vinyl siding,
and broken payphones or bodegas mark nearly every
intersection. I was searching for the apartment of Jay,
Giorgio, and Giuliano—"The Three Brothers," as the
sign above their doorbell said—three I came to find of

only eighty-four others throughout the world who live as they do, following one of the monastic rules modeled after the rule written by the French hermit priest Charles de Foucauld at the beginning of the twentieth century.

Weeks before this day, I had called the Brothers to ask if they would talk to me about Foucauld and their own lives of service and prayer within their monastic order, so different from other monastic communities in that members see it as their calling to work manual or entry-level jobs and live in poor communities, mixing invisibly with the general population. It is important to them not to focus on the type of work they do in and of itself, but to draw closer to people through the daily tasks they perform.

I am an introverted person by nature, and, though the Brothers welcomed me into their modest bi-level apartment like family long awaiting my arrival, I was nervous at having arranged to spend an afternoon and evening with three men I didn't know. These feelings disappeared, though, as soon as I sat down in the communal seating area next to the kitchen with Jay, Giorgio, and Giuliano, three dangerously good listeners, with many questions at hand.

All were in their mid-fifties: Giuliano was professorial in appearance with glasses and a quiet air of concentration; Giorgio exuded the air of everyone's favorite uncle—gregarious on the surface, serious underneath; and Jay, with his store of jokes ("given that there are only eighty-four of us in the entire world, you're pretty lucky to be meeting three of us at once"), possessed the archetypal presence of the eldest brother, one who had gone off into the world and seen it all—older upon return yet having retained an air of youth.

If I were to have encountered these men on the way into work on the subway in the morning, nothing would have indicated that they were monks, just as little in their apartment suggested that I had been received into a monastery. Except for the modest chapel that faced the street and the life-sized photograph of Foucauld on the wall above me—one taken near the end of his life, by which time he'd been transformed into a wizened figure of indeterminate race—their apartment had the air of so many other people's I know in New York. It was clean, tidy, and organized like a boat to make the most of the space. An aluminum espresso maker and international cookbooks sat upon the shelves.

These circumstances in which they lived were part of their calling in following the life of Foucauld, whose great contribution was proposing the importance of imitating Jesus of *Nazareth*—that is, the life of Jesus before he emerged into the public as the Son of God, the life he lived in a village, where he worked in obscurity as a carpenter.

Responding to their questions, I shared some of the highlights of my last few years over cups of espresso as the late afternoon light of winter waned. I told them about my love of painting and Florence and Titian's painting of Margaret in the Uffizi Galleries, explaining how I felt Margaret had appeared to me to deliver the message that I needed to turn more toward the light. I told them how shortly thereafter I decided to follow the saints who appeared to me, trusting they'd come to me for a reason and trying to understand why.

Foucauld, I told them, was first mentioned to me by a priest in Lisieux, France, where I'd gone in search of Thérèse, as a man who inspires those who follow in his footsteps to divide their lives between deep prayer and social action—seemingly irreconcilable, even opposing disciplines. In the year since, Foucauld had cropped up in several other places along my way, and I'd been struck by both the fervid loneliness of his life and the compromised nature of his endeavors. He'd been moved to re-embrace his own faith, Catholicism, for instance, through contact with the deep faith of Islam and yet settled in North Africa with the hope of converting Muslims to Christianity. He clearly admired the nomadic tribes of the Sahara and yet allowed racist attitudes toward them to infiltrate his writings; and he lived a profound life as an ascetic and holy man in the desert while retaining his nationalistic commitment to French colonialism.

While he'd been fully aware of and fully suffered his loneliness, he'd not seemed to realize he led a compromised existence, as blind as any of us are to the paradigm in which he lived and how it shaped his thoughts and perceptions of the world. Compromise, however, had become a frequent topic of discussion among people interested in this man and his great contribution to the modern spiritual landscape.

The Brothers were surprised that I'd found Foucauld peppering my path, as they didn't feel he was a visible or particularly appealing figure in our current time, a reality—understandably enough—that disappointed them. The order based upon his rule was a strange one, they explained—monks and nuns living in small communities on the fringes of society, indistinguishable in their work and dress from the struggling citizenry with whom they lived. More often than not, those drawn to religious vocations these days were seeking stability, foundation, and structure—a withdrawal from the chaotic world in which we live, not an invisible immersion within it. These Brothers, on the other hand, came from an entirely different set of circumstances: They grew up in the more rigid systems of the fifties and were attracted to an unconventional religious order when they came of age in the sixties.

Gathered around the table in focused conversation, the short winter day waned entirely away. Giorgio got up to turn on lamps as Jay described being drawn to the order in his early twenties. The son of a gravedigger and general handyman for the church, he knew he wanted to devote his life to God but to remain firmly planted in the world. He also knew that he wanted "a breath of fresh air" after growing up in a traditional Catholic family on the east coast of the United States in the 1950s. At the age of twenty-four, after a stint in the Navy, he spent a summer volunteering for the Catholic Workers in New York. His exposure to a completely different side of American society galvanized his understanding of what he'd like to do, and, after researching the types of orders that existed, he visited the Little Brothers in New York. At the time, they lived in the East Village near the Bowery, only a few blocks from the Catholic Workers. Although he was fairly certain that he'd like to join the order, he returned to his home in Connecticut to work for his father and contemplate the decision for about nine months before joining the Brothers as a postulant.

Giuliano, meanwhile, had been an architecture student in Florence and, radicalized by workers' demonstrations, left his studies to become a monk.

And lastly, Giorgio had come into contact with poverty in the shantytowns on the outskirts of Rome. The faith of the people he met had touched something deep within him, and he felt that he had no choice but to resign all that was familiar to him and to follow and to learn from their great store of spirituality. Being Italian, both Giuliano and Giorgio were drawn to Foucauld through the profound and beautiful writings of Carlo Carretto, an Italian schoolteacher who traveled to the Sahara Desert in 1954 to enter the novitiate of the Little Brothers of Jesus at the age of forty-four, leaving behind his life in Italy as a well-known Catholic activist.

Jay got up to make dinner, calling over to us as the conversation continued, and to my great fascination the Brothers described their unfolding lives after they joined the order. Giorgio arrived in New York more than twenty years before, lacking a green card, and worked illegally in a pizza parlor during his first years in the United States. He'd also spent several years trying to track down homeless people and deliver their mail to them.

Giuliano spent many years in Japan, laboring in a leather-making factory, at that time and still today considered the job of descendants of "outcasts," a class of people who, though no longer officially discriminated against in Japan, had a status in Japan's medieval caste system similar to that of the untouchables of India.

After spending several months studying French in Canada, Jay spent years working in hothouses in Spain, in an Algerian soda factory as an illegal alien, and, after studies in Italy and Switzerland, as a home health aid in Spain before returning to the United States in 1992. It was through his job as a home health aid, a position he took because it was the only one available to him, that he worked with AIDS patients for the first time and realized that he loved working with people in a social service capacity. Mentioning more than once that life is a process, Jay reminded me of my own feeling of surprise at what had emerged from the decisions I'd made when I myself was eighteen or nineteen, a path I'd chosen without knowing where it would lead, without understanding that we all are in the service of our callings.

And so the conversation ranged over an array of subjects as the evening wore on and the tantalizing scent of Jay's dinner filled the room. Always circling back to Foucauld, we talked about community, art, and the ongoing war in Iraq. As poverty is value-honored by Foucauld and his followers, we also discussed the exorbitant salaries earned by a small proportion of the population while so many people in the United States and throughout the world continue to struggle for basic survival. We talked about the critical presence of poverty in the life of Christ and the spiritual lives of individuals. Jay, an aid at a day center for Alzheimer's and dementia patients at the Grand Army Plaza, described his job caring for men and women who had lost the memory of who they'd once been. This was a tragedy for the families, he said, but to his mind a kind of liberation for the patients themselves, living in the moment, every day fresh and new.

New York City provides transportation to and from school only for troubled and disabled students, and Giorgio, a New York Public School bus driver in Jamaica, Queens, described the children he bused to and from school, the young lives that seemed pre-determined by their time and place. And Giuliano, who helped to distribute food from a mobile unit soup kitchen founded by the Daughters of Charity, described the men they served in some of the poorest and most dangerous neighborhoods of New York—those who would wait in line for lunch, turning whenever they saw a van out of the corner of their eye in eager hope that someone had come to pick up workers for a day job.

While much of our conversation is lost to me now, here are some of the things that stood out:

Giuliano saying that the world needs a man with the charisma of St. Francis, a man capable of inspiring people with a true feeling for the holiness of poverty, and Giorgio saying that they chose to live among the poor not only in the hope of creating an oasis within an urban desert but also for what they could gain from the people whose lives they shared. He pointed out that Foucauld continuously sought to go to the poorest place on earth. From the Trappist monastery of Our Lady of the Snows in France, he went to one in Akbes, Syria. He left the Trappist order and became a solitary servant to the Poor Clare nuns in Palestine, where he lived in a gardening hut. He went to the Sahara, where he was eventually so poor that the people took care of him. He was lonely, waiting year after year for someone to join him there and help to create the monastic community he yearned for. By most standards of measurement, he was a failure: He attracted no followers to speak of and baptized only two people in all his years as a priest. He was compromised, living as a neighbor with the Tuareg people, yet storing French ammunition that could be used against them.

He died like a dog in the early hours of a December morning, as Giorgio said. And why? Because he believed in the power of imitating Christ.

What was the important message of Foucauld for those of us alive today? I asked. The Brothers said it was twofold: his insistence that we cry the gospel with our hearts —live it out from the depths of our beings—and that we search within ourselves for the greatest poverty of spirit, trusting that from that place fruit would be borne.

I retired at around nine to the narrow room downstairs belonging to a Brother who had taken a year's sabbatical. My mind was full of what we had talked of, and I'd drunk too much espresso, and so I lay, neither waking nor sleeping, listening to the sound of the television from upstairs—the Academy Awards—and reflecting on and sifting through our conversation. The lives of the men I met were so human—going to work each day, watching the Academy Awards, digging with mortal enthusiasm into dinner and the pie I'd brought for dessert. Few of the people they met along their day's journey in life would be aware that the lives they lived were focused on God.

I thought of what we had talked of: Each of us is constrained and created by circumstances—elderly people who had forgotten the faces of the children they had given birth to and raised, children whose spirits were drowning in rage, a wealthy French army officer living as an ascetic in the desert—and yet each of us is somehow created for freedom. Each of us is a surprise, with a narrative that is, in the end, somehow inevitable. And each of us is visibly blossoming out of an invisible seed with its preordained patterns, flowering within the specific conditions of our environment.

As the first snow of winter began to fall on New York, I thought of Foucauld in the desert of Algeria, trying to understand why he had gone there, saddened by the thought of his terrible solitude and uncertain as to why or what I myself was searching for. I felt sad, yet whole, as the snow, glittering under the streetlight, fell thicker, and the radiator under the window gurgled.

In the morning, we gathered in the chapel for an hour of group Adoration before each of us went our own way. On the third floor of the apartment facing busy Palmetto Street, the Brothers had created a sanctuary with the most modest—even ordinary—of resources that, though modern and very American, equaled, to my mind, the simple serenity of the Romanesque chapels I visited in France. With its plastic Venetian blinds at the window, nondescript blue carpeting on the floor, pale neutral walls with a hint of orange, and white trim, the chapel breathed with an air of balance, harmony, and the multicultural roots from which it sprang.

On the wall between the two windows at the front of the room a small crucifix hung above the Host, the wood of the cross fashioned from the thin branches of a tree, the painted plaster figure of Christ filled with empathetic suffering. A copy of Andrei Rublyev's *Trinity* and a Madonna in muted tones of gray and blue imparted a further feeling of refined beauty. Candles burned steadily in the stillness, a halo of luminous light in a room otherwise dim on this gray winter morning. Clay bowls for burning incense were placed on the floor, each of them emitting a small curl of smoke, imparting the room with an essence of earth and matter. It was Jay's turn to open the Morning Prayer. He tapped on the gong, and as the resonance of the *om* faded away, he began reading about Martin Luther King's life from Robert Ellsberg's book *All Saints*, his voice rich with the sound of the words, mellifluous with the story he conveyed, the story of a life that appeared seamless on the surface, inevitable in its flow, like a river now that its narrative was complete, beginning to end.

The sensitivity of the Brothers, the atmosphere of the chapel, and the presence of Foucauld himself—the nearly life-sized picture of him in the other room with the symbolic depiction on the chest of his white robe of a red cross growing out of a heart—encouraged openness. I tried to listen with my heart, following those things that struck me more than others, to see where I was being taken. In particular, Jay related how Martin Luther King's public life as we know it began when Rosa Parks was arrested for refusing to relinquish her seat to a white man on a Montgomery, Alabama, bus. I knew little about Rosa Parks on that morning as Jay read, other than her name and the act of courage for which she is known, and found myself wondering what had fueled her resistance to injustice. What had caused her to stand up for what she knew was right? Later, "Googling" her name on the Internet, I would discover that she was not just weary from a long day's work but was tired of being treated as a second-class citizen and had been living an active life in pursuit of justice long before she was arrested at the age of forty-two. She was yet another person whose act of courage grew out of her faith in God.

King, though, was twenty-six, and fresh out of graduate school in Boston, Jay read, when he addressed a packed church in Montgomery: "There comes a time when people get tired of being trampled over by the iron feet of oppression. . . ." Only two years later as the Civil Rights Movement gained momentum, he received death threats over the phone and sat in his kitchen over a cup of coffee, contemplating withdrawing from the fight, agonizing about his safety and that of his family. Entrusting himself to God as he sat at the kitchen table, he immediately heard a voice telling him to "stand up for righteousness. Stand up for justice. Stand up for truth. And lo, I will be with you, even until the end of the world."

It was hardly more than a decade later, the night before he was assassinated, that King gave a speech showing how far he'd come in courage. Addressing the possibility of being killed because of what he believed in, he said he accepted such a fate were it to be his, for God had led him to the top of the mountain and showed him the promised land—poignant words, so strikingly juxtaposed to those Jay had read a few minutes earlier about King having been afraid of dying for the cause. Though his house was bombed, though he was jailed, stabbed, and vilified, he retained his faith and was given the strength to face anything by the voice he heard that night in his kitchen.

I closed my eyes, considering Rosa Parks, Martin Luther King, and the conversation I'd had with Giorgio,

Jay, and Giuliano the previous day. It was impossible not to see a connection between Parks, King, and the saints I'd spent the past year of my life studying, for Parks and King embodied a direct, contemporary, living example of profound faith and the certain direction it imposes on a life regardless of the consequences. Both had heard God speaking to them—King literally in the kitchen of his house that night; both had acted with great courage in seeking to accomplish what they felt called to undertake, and, in the case of King, martyrdom was accepted as the necessary ramification of standing up for a new vision of justice in a world where old values and prejudices reigned.

The sensations of the world pulled me out of my reverie—the itch on my arm; the smell of incense; one of the Brothers in the room shifting; someone shoveling the sidewalk outside—the familiar sound of the metal head of a shovel scraping against pavement at regular, rhythmic intervals; buses slowing, then revving their motors in harmony with the general urban din. These sensations, along with Rosa Parks and Martin Luther King, the three Brothers, Foucauld, my efforts, and the efforts of all the people outside on the street striving to live their lives fully, swirled together in an interconnected harmony. I was grateful to the Brothers for the oasis they provided, an echo of a distant desert, their home a place where there existed a hint of what one must sense under the sky of the Sahara: the great expanse of creation, a timeless but contemporaneous expanse where I felt nothing but breathing, quietly, listening within the labor of my days. Within the vast appetite of existence and ambition, we forget sometimes the beauty of hospitality—a shared bowl of rice, conversation, prayer, an acknowledgment of our common ground.

I still wasn't sure why I had visited the Brothers or was fascinated and moved by Foucauld. Jay, Giorgio, and Giuliano had replenished in me, though, a faith that the efforts of everyday life, the efforts of everyday people blossom fully in time. Thinking of the Brothers, of Rosa Parks, of King, of Foucauld, feeling the visible and invisible emanations of their lives reaching out into the universe, I sensed the vital sources of life to be found in the most seemingly barren places. What can any of us know of our contribution to others' lives, of the fruits of our labor, or the reach of our influence? Foucauld died after a life of poverty and compromise, in a far corner of the Sahara Desert, but a century later he lives on not only in my own conscious mind and life but also now in yours, too.

mortal saints and immortal callings

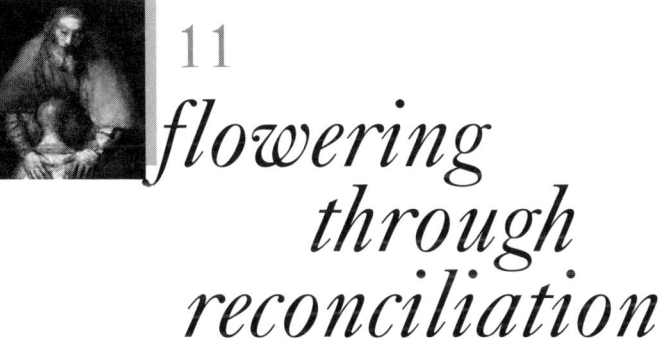

11

flowering through reconciliation

SAINT RITA OF CASCIA

When we are busy, or suffering persecutions or trials, when
we cannot get as much quiet as we should like, and at
seasons of aridity, we have a very good Friend in Christ.
We...think of His moments of weakness and times
of trial; and He becomes our Companion.

ST. TERESA OF ÁVILA

IT HAS BEEN SAID THAT RITA OF CASCIA, THE PEACEMAKER, the patron saint of impossible causes, searches for those who are in need of her, finding them on buses, in churches, walking down the street—wherever those may be who feel their situations are hopeless, their lives beyond repair, lost, grieving, embroiled in disputes, suffering from illness, wrapped in the darkness of drugs and alcohol.

For nearly three years I had lived in southern Europe, visiting churches, contemplating the saints, yet I'd not had the opportunity to acquaint myself with Rita (or she to acquaint herself with me) until just before what was to become a tumultuous return to the United States. As I walked the streets of Paris saying good-bye to the beautiful years I'd spent studying painting and writing, sorry to be leaving my life in France behind, Rita appeared to me for the first time, as if to prepare me for the difficult times ahead. Standing in the shadowy chapel of a small nondescript church, she presented herself draped in marble robes, arrayed with a panoply of hand-written salutations thanking her for the miracles she'd wrought.

Even though I knew little about her at the time, I traced my eyes irresistibly over the heartfelt salutations and I understood, in a distant way, that she had helped these people mend the broken shards of their lives, to overcome disappointment, to flower through love when they thought their lives deserts where nothing more would grow.

"You, who know difficulty, you who know the pain of hope, you, saint of the impossible, give me the courage to trust again . . ." a prayer to her began.

The pain of hope. This phrase, these seemingly incompatible words—pain and hope—stuck with me during my first days back in the United States. We all have challenges we struggle with, situations to overcome that only we can feel in their full depth, and, for me, the source of my difficulties was the desire to write and paint when lacking the resources to do so. It is hard to believe in the importance of doing what we must for love alone, to follow our "bliss," as Joseph Campbell encourages, when confronted with no hot water, nights peppered with the sound of gunfire in a dangerous neighborhood, a job in an office as a temp, no health insurance.

As if my struggles had shot a flare up through the spiritual ether, Rita surfaced in my life again, once when I picked up a map at the tourist center on Market Street and noticed a bold arrow pointing to the "National Shrine of Saint Rita of Cascia" in, of all places, South Philly, and then, again, shortly thereafter, when out of the blue, a woman in the office where I worked stopped by my desk and mentioned to me her devotions to Sts. Rita and Jude, companion saints of impossible causes. She showed me the prayer cards she kept with her at all times and urged me to visit the South Philly shrine, repository of a relic of Rita's that had been installed by poor Italian immigrants at the beginning of the twentieth century.

Born in 1377 in a small town in Italy, Rita lived the life of a woman whose many sorrows stand as reminder that life is rarely as bad as it could be.

As was the case for most women of that time, the two options that lay open to her when she came to maturity at the young age of twelve, the same options that Teresa of Ávila faced a hundred and fifty years later, were the convent, or marriage and motherhood. Though Rita wished to become a nun and join the Augustinian convent near her home, her parents did not support her choice of vocation. This, it seems, has remained a common thread, a common hurdle to overcome, in search of defining our vocational paths. It wasn't that they were unsympathetic to her wishes, but that they were concerned about her future welfare, wanting their daughter's life to be secure in a period of time when the Church was faltering under the pressure of the Great Schism.[2] With unrest reverberating even in the religious orders of Rita's hometown, marriage, to her parents, was the safer of the two options.

Rita deferred to her parents' wishes at age fourteen, by marrying the man they'd chosen, and it was because of that fateful day that many years of suffering and loss were to follow. Whether true or not we will never know, but much has been written about the abusiveness and infidelity of her husband.[3] We can be certain that her marriage ended in tragedy when her husband was murdered, the victim of a generations-old feud between his family and another. We can also be certain that her sons perished in the plague, though we will never know if it is true, as has been written, that this was because she asked God to prevent them from avenging their father's death, as they planned. Many interpret their deaths as God's answer to Rita's prayer—taking her sons to keep them from committing murder and bringing mortal sin upon themselves.

Following the loss of her family, Rita remembered her early dream of becoming a nun and, now aged thirty-two, she again sought to join the Augustinian convent. The nuns refused to admit her—she presumed that this was because she was growing older and had borne two children. Sequestering herself in prayer, she remained convinced that her "second calling" was a true one, and once again presented herself at the doors of the convent. This time, the nuns divulged that they feared that Rita, by virtue of having married into a family vendetta, might carry a murderous conflict into the convent, thus disturbing its peaceful walls.

Including the time when she was twelve, Rita had three times sought to enter the convent and three times had failed: She wondered, as any of us would, if she'd been mistaken in believing that she was truly called to become a nun. Many of us seem to instinctively believe that if we are meant to do something, a way will surely be found ("if there's a will, there's a way"), and so Rita wondered if the obstacles to her path remained because she'd misinterpreted her second calling. Yet, though her desires had on three occasions been thwarted, she felt certain that she was meant to encloister herself, and for the fourth time she presented herself before the nuns.

By this point, she was essentially living like a nun in a lay state: She spent many hours each day sequestered in prayer, offered hospitality to strangers and travelers, had accepted the death of her husband and sons without bitterness toward God, had even forgiven her husband's murderers. One would think that on this, her fourth visit to the convent, the nuns, seeing her certainty that

God had "invited" her to join their order, would have relented and welcomed her into the fold. Yet this time, too, they refused her, and—in what must have been a severe blow—they also told her not to ask such a thing of them ever again. Imagine: after several attempts to gain admittance to the hallowed walls of one's vocation (school, internship, profession, job), one is all but told that one's hopes and dreams will never be fulfilled and the only thing to do is to give up. In what appeared to me at the time the understated words of one of her biographers: "It was difficult [for Rita] to reconcile the hard reality of their rejection with the certainty she had of God's will."

Only after four years of struggle did she finally understand that she was called to accomplish a difficult task before she could be admitted to the convent. The nuns had already given her a hint of what it would be, but the sudden presence of St. John the Baptist, St. Augustine of Hippo, and St. Nicholas of Tolentino as she prayed one day bore the message more clearly. They gave her to understand that, while she herself had extended forgiveness to the family of her husband's murderers, the destructive feud wore on between the two families, and it was for her to bring peace to them. Serving as a mediator between her husband's family and the family of his murderers, she convinced them to lay aside their hostility and live in friendship with one another.

Again, Rita presented herself at the doors of the convent, a signed agreement of peace from her family-in-law in

mortal saints and immortal callings

hand, and she was finally welcomed into the community she'd so long sought to enter. She was thirty-six years old, and would live forty years behind the convent walls without record or note until, fifteen years before her death, her forehead was pierced with the wound of one of Christ's thorns.

I did eventually visit Rita's shrine, precipitated by an unexpected event one evening in late winter when I was riding the bus home with a friend. The long and icy fingers of winter continued to grip the city even though spring was near. Dirty snow lay in clumps along the sides of the roads, mirror-like sheets of ice lacquered the sidewalks, and a chill wind chafed and lashed all that it touched. At the Market Street stop, the equatorial commercial belt of Center City separating north from south, all of the white people got off the bus except my friend and me. At the next stop a group of teenagers pushed on board through the rear door.

One of the girls began talking and gesticulating derisively about "white people." I paid no attention. Racial tension boils just under the surface of daily life in Philly and already even the most vitriolic slurs had begun to blend into the general urban din for me. Through the mud-spattered windows my eyes tracked the demographic shift from affluence, to less affluence, to poverty, south to north, the bus lurching slowly from one block to the next. Someone tugged at my hat and hair from behind. A second pull, harder. I glanced around to see a small, impassive-looking adolescent boy. "Don't look at me," he shrugged.

Moments later, there was another yank at my hair, and someone snatched the hat off my head, throwing it into a puddle of muddy water on the floor.

One of the girls leaned in close to my face and wanted to know if I was scared. I didn't think that I was, but I was most certainly at a loss as to how to react, her eyes eager for confrontation, inflamed with juvenile power. Her friends poked at me, slapping the back of my head, some standing in front, smiling sarcastically. "Scared yet?" she asked. As if we'd all agreed to show caution, not a single adult on the crowded bus spoke, the children dangerous just under the surface, reckless in their numbers and youth.

This confrontation, like seeding clouds for rain, led me to the shrine of Rita. Since she was the saint of reconciliation, it seemed appropriate to be drawn to her shrine through the presence of divisiveness—almost as if the event on the bus were a push from Rita herself, a more insistent invitation.

I stepped into the church to find myself greeted by a statue of St. Rocco—or Roch, as I knew him from my travels in France—off in a room to a side where a dozen or so other saints gathered. The patron saint of travelers and the plague-stricken, Roch left his wealthy French family to become a pilgrim, returning home after many

mortal saints and immortal callings

years such a different man that, unrecognized, he was thrown into jail. Between his years as a pilgrim and his return home, he nursed victims of the plague, a role he came to embrace as part of his calling. He suffered a wound and upon realizing it would not heal, withdrew from the world to live as a hermit, attended faithfully by a dog that he'd picked up on his travels.

I wondered why, of all the saints, he, a relatively "small" French saint, was one of the dozen to merit a spot here in this Philadelphia church. Was it because he'd traveled so far from home, and the Italian immigrants who'd built this church, having also traveled so far from home, resonated with his fate? Adorned with scallop shells, a sign of his pilgrimage to St. James's shrine in the Spanish city of Santiago de Compostela, he lifts his tunic to reveal the lesion above his knee, the wound I contemplated many times in chapels devoted to him in France, wondering what its symbolic significance might be—that suffering is a condition of mortality? His dog stands next to him with a small piece of bread in its mouth, Roch gazing into the distance. Did he see, as did I, the beautiful roads of pilgrimage that lay behind him? Those roads lay far, far outside the circumference of this city. Or did he long, as did I, to go back?

To be greeted by Roch, this saint I knew well from my travels, affirmed for me the significance of my having been drawn to the shrine. He was in company with many others I knew from my time in Europe: Thérèse of Lisieux with her bundle of roses; Michael standing astride the demon; Lucy, holding her eyes on a tray; Anne, with her daughter, the Virgin Mary, at her knees. There were also saints from the Americas, such as Our Lady of Guadalupe, who sang a "mellow and delightful" song to attract Juan Diego, a converted Indian. Mother Frances Cabrini appeared stern with the great will she must have possessed when, turned away as a novice at two convents in Italy, she took a private vow of virginity and founded a small community of sisters of her own. Martin de Porres, the illegitimate son of an ex-slave and a knight, who nursed the sick and poor of Lima, Peru—*all* the sick and poor, regardless of race—looked as gentle in his sculpture as I have imagined him to be, based on the stories I've read of his selfless ministry and compassion.

Together, they represented many generations of human life working tirelessly to fulfill their callings, persevering through weariness and internal trials, retaining faith and hope in adverse conditions, leaving for us their gifts of insight: the beauty of smallness, the need to protect sacred places, to care tenderly for life, and to work to alleviate injustice, along with a whole host of other virtues clarified within the vessels of lives lived well.

Entering the main area of the lower church, I took my seat on one of the pews that encircled a statue of Rita. Her shrine was peaceful, with the larger-than-life-size statue of the saint in a dramatic posture of supplication. Her long life was one of struggle redeemed through faith. Her vocation, saint of reconciliation, grew out of the many and varied schisms she healed of necessity when confronted with circumstances she neither willed nor desired. The olive branch that she extended to her husband's murderer symbolized the peace she achieved in the face of great loss, and shared with those who were less inclined by nature to forgive. Perhaps the circular design of the seating referred, symbolically, to wholeness, the wholeness we achieve through reconciliation. The configuration of the space seemed a fitting tribute to her life and to her femininity, while at the same time creating a feeling of enclosed privacy, an enclave in which the sharing of confidences, the intimate moment of asking this woman to intercede on our behalf, was still and safe. It was a place where, should we not yet know what to do but expose the depths of our suffering, there would be time for our thoughts to form.

Father di Gregorio, rector of the shrine, in reflecting upon Rita's vast popularity as an intercessor, suggested that it's hard for many of us to imagine approaching a saint with the stature of Augustine or Teresa of Ávila with requests that may seem small, while Rita invites our most tender petitions. A wife before she was a nun, a mother who suffered the death of her sons, a woman compelled to forgive her husband's murderer and one whose mortal suffering provided her with a mystical connection with Christ, she seems closer to us in what she experienced than many of the other saints, more understanding of life's ordinary challenges.

A steady stream of people, men and women of all races and ages, came in off the street to sit in her presence, some for just a minute or two, others settling in for what appeared to be an extended visit, some visibly praying, others in quiet meditation. And, curiously enough, a guard stood by protecting her, a man in a uniform who watched and who I first mistook for one of us—though, in hindsight, maybe he was. . . .

A movie I once saw by the Russian filmmaker Andrei Tarkovsky came to mind. In Tarkovsky's film, a man called "the stalker" is paid to guide groups of people through "the zone" to a spring that lies in the midst of a desolate plain. In this zone, at this spring, those who have paid the price of passage will have their most desired wish granted to them—if, that is, they have the courage to ask. Few do, as it turns out, for along the way, the stalker tells the story of a man who'd gone there to pray that his wealthy brother would recover from serious illness, only to discover upon returning home that his brother had died while he was away, leaving him his fortune.

I think of this movie often now in relation to Rita, if for no other reason than that she is reputed to exact a high price for her intercession: Those who receive through the gift of her beneficence are said to suffer a proportionate loss. Many hesitate to call upon her out of fear, but Father di Gregorio believes this legend can, or should, be more figuratively understood. There are times, he said, that we approach God with "clenched hands" and "full petitions. . . . Sometimes, we have to drop what we have in order to receive."

I contemplated the images that have come to be associated with Rita: bees, the bees found covering her face and chest once when she slept as an infant, crawling into her open mouth; and roses, the rose discovered blooming in the winter in the garden of the house she'd shared with her family as a young woman. Both images bore fruitful connotations—honey, blossoming; yet both evoked suffering and loss—the sting of a bee, vulnerability in the cold.

It was not concern over the rumor of a heavy price to be paid that compelled me to sit in front of her and ask for nothing. I like to think that it was, rather, uncertainty and confusion within myself over what indeed I had the right to ask. But maybe they are one and the same—certainty and lack of fear. Which is to say, perhaps when we no longer fear the prospect of having to pay a price, no matter how high, for what it is that we ask, it is only then that we are truly in need.

The one thing I was not fearful of asking for, as the prayer I'd read in Paris had articulated, was to embrace the pain of continuing to hope during this period of transition. But hope did not seem enough to me at that moment, so instead of making a request, I sat, hoping in the depths of my consciousness that by merely visiting Rita I would be given what I needed, whatever that might be.

Like tender, fresh shoots pulled from a hothouse into the chill, spring air, I stepped out of the church, walked across the street to a twenty-four-hour diner, and took a seat at the counter. Customers were herded to the exit perforce through a passageway formed of tubular chrome railings, orchestrated to ensure a stop at the cash register. The cashier, an old woman, sat behind bulletproof glass, the surface of which was covered with hand-written notes: *To all/customers/we will not/except any/travelers cheques. . . . All credit/cards will be/subject to/Proper I.D./NO EXCEPTIONS.*

The waitress, a woman in her late sixties, I guessed, had an unforced downward turn to her mouth and took in a visible breath when I gave her my order for tea— "Yes, only tea," I said. I sat holding the warm mug between my hands, elbows resting on the counter, the essence of black tea and fresh lemon slice pricking my senses. A pyramid of miniature Kellogg's cereal boxes filled a shelf across from me. I began to feel more comfortable—familiar territory, this diner. As the waitress took orders from other customers, I could not help smiling at the charm and eccentricity with which she engaged her world. To the woman who asked to substitute potatoes for fishcakes, she said, "no substitutions"; to the woman who asked if she could have fried catfish, "not on Sundays"; to the man who chose two veggie sides with his spare rib platter, "just comes with one." There was a beauty, both to the questions being asked— the anticipated pleasures they implied—and the waitress's terse but rhythmic replies, a shuttlecock of interaction, a dance of human connectivity no less warm or loving for its nature.

She wore an Eagles cap and a little pink ribbon, and I imagined her rooting the Eagles on to victory and praying for the plight of women afflicted with breast cancer. In her I saw hope, a hope that a cure would be found, hope that the hometown team would take away a hard-earned Super Bowl victory even though they hadn't for so many years and their star player was recovering from an injury. Was it not in a desire to share with the community that she emblazoned herself with signs of solidarity, a mother lode of warmth beneath a thin protective veneer? Under what circumstances would the tenderness in her break through—flowers through the parched winter earth? It certainly couldn't be easy to stand on her feet and work the crowds all day.

For my part, I realized that I probably didn't seem all that warm to her on first glance, either—silently jotting down my thoughts in a journal, placing what must have seemed a miserly order for tea (read: small tip), avoiding the coconut pound cake that begged to be eaten from under its transparent plastic shield. Any instinct toward friendliness I might have had circled under the cloud cover of what I perceived to be her gruff exterior. She must have sensed me watching, though, for she turned my way, and I smiled. She didn't exactly smile in return but did ask if I wanted more hot water, glancing at the squished-up teabag that lay on the saucer by my cup—a significant leap forward in our relationship.

"You a writer?" she asked when she refilled my cup. After a moment's hesitation, I said yes. "Published?" she asked, a question I'd once hated. "Yes," I said. "My nephew's a writer," she said. "He tells me it's not easy." Another customer came in, and she turned from me, her gruff charm returning. "Not today," I heard her say. Notwithstanding the obstacles in my path, I realized that I could not in fact conceive of any life for myself other than that of striving to become a writer and painter. This being so, I had no choice but to believe that with patience and in time the reason for the impediments I faced would become clear to me. Certainly my struggles had put me into contact with experiences that would never have been mine had circumstances been different, and so maybe, probably, the difficulties I faced were meant to neither deter me from my path, nor to test me—as we so often think when we face resistance. Rather, maybe the obstacles confronted me with a challenge that, if met, would unlock the door to the place I wished to enter.

I looked around through the din of shuffled platters and chit-chat. After a lifetime of travel, I ushered Philly into my heart, a new city for me, not one in which I ever would have expected to live. Yet, lost in reverie about our interconnected fates, I had a sudden feeling of inevitability, having come to live in a city that needed so badly to be reconciled just at the moment when I could see that I did too.

12
protecting
high places

SAINT MICHAEL

The great angel Michael always interceding

for the human race...

TESTAMENTS OF THE TWELVE PATRIARCHS

THE HISTORY AND BELIEFS THAT SURROUND THE ARCHANGEL Michael are as many and varied as the years are long since the first record of his story. A brief synopsis from Butler's *Lives of the Saints* begins with the tenth and twelfth chapters of the Book of Daniel, referring to him as "one of the chief princes." Considered to have had the closest relation to God of all the archangels, he is perhaps best known for his battle, and eventual victory, over the great dragon—"the old serpent who is called the devil himself and Satan"—banishing him from heaven. It was Michael who reconciled Abraham to the necessity of death, and it is he who serves as the scribe to record all the deeds of humanity in the books of Heaven. And it was Michael who fought with the devil over the body of Moses, though when Michael was overcome with wrath, he withdrew deferentially, allowing God to rebuke the devil.

In mid-September, 2004, Michael's already complex and paradoxical presence gained new meaning for me as the great protector of life itself. I was just outside of Leon, Spain, resting and seeking refuge for a few hours while on the pilgrimage route to Santiago de Compostela. High above a baroque altarpiece that stood majestically within the church of La Virgen del Camino, Michael braces himself on one knee while lunging forward, opposite foot planted on the floor, body squared in a single unified gesture, his sword raised with authority above his head.

With unflinching sureness, he is preparing to slay the dragon that threatens to encroach upon the sacred shrine of the Virgen del Camino, a sixteenth-century depiction in wood of the Pietà, marking the spot where, in 1505, the Virgin appeared to a simple shepherd.

It became clear to me at that moment that the Virgen del Camino not only was nurturing the baby Jesus but also was a symbol of life itself, and that the grand *retablo* behind the altar could be seen as an enactment of the great drama between good and evil, the importance of protecting high places. Insofar as our vocations are a creative act (which it seems to me they are) and Mary symbolic of the ultimate act of creation, the figures that stood before me represented an ancient but still living model of the forces

mortal saints and immortal callings

at play in our everyday lives. Mary, inwardly turned, focused on the matter at hand, oblivious to both the serpent and Michael above—a demeanour, a way of being, that we can look to as we define and pursue our vocational paths: focused, devoted, at one with our efforts, concerned not by that which threatens.

When I came upon the Virgen del Camino, I had been on the pilgrim's trail for nearly two months, in search of, among other things, the hope, or faith, to continue following my path in life. From the first steps I'd taken out of Le Puy en Velay in France, I had encountered images of Michael. After attending the Pilgrim's Benediction at the cathedral consecrated to the "Black Virgin" of Le Puy, I had climbed to the top of a volcanic peak high above the town, where a tenth-century chapel dedicated to Michael, carved out of the soft stone, lay half-ruined. A small troupe of restorers was carefully clearing away centuries of debris to reveal the fading images of the archangel. Michael's eyes stared out at me from the otherwise indiscernible fresco. At nearly every church and chapel along the way, I also found him watching. Indeed, Michael and the Virgin Mary, the protector of heaven and the symbol of life itself, were daily companions as I'd walked across France and Spain toward St. James's shrine on the Galician coast in northwestern Spain.

In every image I'd seen of Michael—whether already having thrust the sword into the dragon's mouth or preparing to do so—he displays a fierce, though measured power. In this regard, his demeanor as he confronts the dragon is very unlike that of Margaret of Antioch's, beseechingly turned to the heavens for help, determined to prevail, though visibly horrified by the demon that confronts her.

In graceful counterpoint to Margaret, Michael displays no hesitation, only sureness of purpose. He looks not at the dragon as he raises his sword but straight ahead—at us, at me, at you—a resolute and steady gaze that appears with startling consistency throughout the ages, in the simple stone bas-reliefs of the Middle Ages, in Byzantine icons and crumbling frescoes, and in the naturalistically rendered masterpieces of the Renaissance, speaking in silence of that for which only action will suffice. His expression is that of a man intent on impressing upon us the importance of the task—a task from which, were he to fail, would follow sure death. "Now, look," he seems to say, "this is what and how you are to do what you are to do. Sometimes it is necessary to strike swiftly at that which threatens the creative force of life."

As I'd walked toward Santiago, I had slowly, layer by layer, been unpeeled, stripped to my core. During the hours on the road, putting one foot in front of the other, I had come to remember the hurtful things I'd done toward others and been sorry for them. I'd found the need to let go— of possessions and presumptions, competitive urges, and egoistic aims. I'd just crossed the long, desert-like *meseta* of Spain, and, sitting at the shrine outside of Leon, I felt yet another layer of myself—the residue of disappointing times when I'd been slighted and mocked by others when

mortal saints and immortal callings

I'd shared my work or goals—peeled away and exposed to the earth and sky. Perhaps we all experience moments when the sanctuary of our vocations are encroached upon, when people smile a bit disbelievingly, a bit derisively, as we tell them of our plans and our dreams, and then our witnesses shrug their shoulders and say, "Perhaps. . . ." What are we to do when we are told that our stories don't work, that we might as well give up, that we are too old to attend medical school, that we don't or will never measure up to our peers or predecessors in a program?

It is easy to allow these kinds of judgments to infiltrate our sense of purpose, sometimes altogether obliterating it, leaving us to abandon our paths. Are we, I wondered that morning in Leon, to do as Michael does and strike down the enemy when we sense those sacred places within us being encroached upon? The answer can only be no, my better half responds.

Daylight faded to dusk as I sat at the foot of the Virgen del Camino, contemplating his presence, Michael with his sword raised in perpetuity. An incident years before when I was living in Prague surfaced to my conscious mind. It was a spring afternoon, the crispy, blue kind that is so welcome after a long, dark winter. A large group of people, myself included, were quietly stretched out on the warm concrete when a drunk, powerfully built man began to belt out a sad love ballad, circling round and round the fountain in the center of the square, closing his eyes with emotion, holding his hand to his mouth as if his fist were a microphone.

Another man approached and began to mimic him, laughing, and in very short order a fight broke out between the two. Those of us present watched with increasing attention as the altercation grew more serious, progressing from insults to fisticuffs. The man who had been singing was much stronger than the other, and, despite his drunkenness, succeeded in throwing his adversary to the ground. Triumphantly, he pinned him with a booted foot to the chest, and as he loomed over his defeated opponent, prepared to kick him in the head with his steel toe.

All of us, each and every person in the square, rose and moved instinctively forward with a collectively shouted "No!" Snapped out of his drunken rage, the victor drew back from the blow that could very well have killed the other man—his fury occasioned, I have no doubt, by feeling exposed, the tender thread of his heart threatened by ridicule.

Even then and to this day, the scene in the square impressed and troubled me, both for obvious and perhaps not-so-obvious reasons. I felt awe that we all had acted as one to thwart the mortal blow that threatened the defeated man. It was the right thing to do.

Yet even at the time there had been, I felt, another side to what had transpired. If we as the public had the right to protect the man who lay prostrate on the ground, didn't the man who had been singing have the right to defend himself from ridicule? Had we simply prevented him from justly driving the sword into the serpent's mouth, vanquishing that which threatened?

mortal saints and immortal callings

I will confess that that day I sympathized, even identified, with the man as he'd gone round and round the fountain in the square, singing his song. Not a day goes by where I don't witness, both in my own life and others, the humiliating and destructive force that words can wield. In the broadest sense, all of us strive to sing our songs in life and must do so, often, before the harshest of critics. What are we to do to protect ourselves?

Above the altarpiece in front of me, the dragon twisted and writhed as the blade pierced its throat, jaws thrashing in desperate defiance of inevitable defeat. And it was without rage, or hatred, or blood lust that Michael laid witness to and vanquished that which must not be.

Perhaps it is not for us to fight. Perhaps it is better for us to stay focused, concentrating on the task at hand, and allow Michael, seraph, high archangel, to intervene on our behalf as he so clearly did that beautiful spring day in Prague.

13

pietà

THE VIRGIN MARY

For I have already told you that suffering and
sorrow increase in proportion to love...

St. Catherine of Siena

Having been back from a two-and-a-half-year sojourn in Europe for several months now, I flip through a thick stack of postcards I collected while there, postcards bearing the image of the Virgin Mary. I look out of the window of my Philadelphia apartment into this misty, spring dawn, as if searching for her face on the wall of the decaying brick tenement across the way.

One of the many important things that Europe demonstrates, I came to feel, is that the presence of the Holy Mother can be found in any number of odd places—in front of a war cemetery, in the parking lot of an abattoir, at the foundation of a great cathedral, in a rocky grotto or sheep meadow, or standing resolutely in a traffic circle swarming with late afternoon rush-hour traffic. Like grass breaking through concrete in this North Philly neighborhood, so Mary's presence was in Europe, a reminder of the persistence and indefatigability of life. Mary, called to usher in new life in all its many forms, a model of motherhood, constantly reaffirmed the importance of maternal care: selflessness, generosity, kindness, forgiveness, and a concern for the good of all. In the face of the most brutal realities of our human condition, she remained tender as the rain that fell softly when I slept last night, as tender as life and that which lives must be.

Pope John Paul II believed that the vocation of women, as understood through Mary, would re-humanize a world dominated by hedonism and materialism. In his "*Gospel of Life*" he calls upon women to "teach others that human relations are authentic if they are open to accepting the other person: a person who is recognized and loved because of the dignity which comes from being a person and not from other considerations, such as usefulness, strength, intelligence, beauty or health." This contribution of women is "an indispensable prerequisite for an authentic cultural change," for replacing, as one writer has said, "the culture of death with the civilization of love." In her writings on vocation, Edith Stein saw in Mary a model of what it would mean to "feminize" the professions, all professions: that is, for both men and women to practice their work with a concrete concern for the feelings and welfare of others.

It is windy out, and perhaps it is this that obscures the stillness in which she would otherwise appear—if not as a vision in front of me, then as a sensation within. If not physically then spiritually—stilling the uneasiness I woke with this morning, inspiring me with faith that *feeling* and *tenderness* is the matter of creation, the matter of daily life, softening the hard edges of reason and conflict.

The branches of trees rake and scrape against one another outside my window, and an American flag drapes down over the entrance of the post office, snapping back and forth. A black plastic grocery bag, long trapped in the branches of a tree, fills with air like a sail, tugging to free itself from its net of brittle wood. These images are far removed from what I now dimly remember of rural France, the churches of southern Europe, candles flickering within their stone refuge, the peal of morning bells ringing precisely at seven AM— announcing the procession of bells that will chime on the hour until midnight falls. I am surprised by this, my longing, but I found it easier there, somehow, to lay down the weapons of wit, quip, and logic, to stand unguarded in the world.

At this very moment, at the ragged tail end of winter, it seems that everything beautiful must have happened in some other time and place. I know this is not true, though. Even in tattered North Philly there is beauty. The challenge is to have the vision to see it, the courage, or faith, to believe in it, as Mary saw and believed in the beauty of the dirty and illiterate peasant children, the grieving, the sick, and the lame to whom she has appeared over the centuries. Here at this very moment—as a plane passes overhead, a homeless man hobbles by, and the

mortal saints and immortal callings

neighbor's dog rummages through the splayed bags of trash on the sidewalk—even here, is beauty, and a world that needs our most precious creations.

Though it is as fully light as it will become today, the morning is dim under a dense shelf of cloud cover. Most of the cars driving past push forward through the thick air with their headlights still on, as if in procession to a funeral. The weather-worn bamboo wind chimes hanging from the bare branch of the tree in the empty lot below fills my room with the faint, organic, and nearly inaudible sound of ritual, a call to prayer in the distant Himalayas, a call to prayer on an overcast Philadelphia morning. There is a tragic undertow to the dilapidated Red Ryder wagon half-buried in the earth beneath the tree, handle sticking up, evoking the final pages of Melville's *Moby Dick*, Queegqueg's hand surfacing to nail a bird to the mast of the ship as it, and everyone on it, sank into the surging and unknowable fathoms that awaited them having pursued the destruction of a whale to their own demise. As the wagon and Melville, the gift of his great works, are a reminder of time passing, time past, such are these post-cards of the holy Mary, mother of God, of life renewed.

The tragic undertow that can press against us—the first week of this month, March 2005, when twenty-two people were murdered in this "City of Brotherly Love"—seems worth mentioning, worth remembering, as much as the two and a half years I spent in Europe becoming acquainted with that mystical spiritual epicenter, the tempering and wordless presence of Mary, especially as it is the tragic undertow she so often redeems. Of these twenty-two fatalities, one was a young child standing on the street beside his mother, waiting for the bus as a stray bullet ripped through the flesh and bone of his ribcage, sending him away from this world we know.

I look down at the image on one of my cards, the small, painted wood fifteenth-century "*Vierge de douleur*" I saw at the Abbey church in Moissac, a town in France that had been a major pilgrims' halt during the Middle Ages. Head tilted, eyes closed, Mary appears drawn, tired, and older than in any other image I've seen of her. I am struck by how remarkably akin she looks to many of the women I see on the buses in Philadelphia. I leaf through my tattered pile of cards once again: images of Mary holding Christ the King, both she and the preternaturally mature infant wearing golden crowns, Rembrandt's painting of the young, very human Mary glancing from her book to her child's face as she rocks his wicker bassinet, the small painting of the Annunciation in the Louvre, attributed to Leonardo—her surprise at the visit of the angel Gabriel who has come to call her to service, dawn breaking on the distant horizon, the dark silhouette of trees heavy against a pale morning sky.

Tenderness and love, feeling, a sensation of grace flowing hand to heart and back again, a stepping back to allow room for the less fortunate, the less strong: as Edith Stein writes, Mary reveals to us the emotion at the center of the soul, that would transmute daily life were it to enter into the work we do.

It seems now clear in her relative absence, the power of her figure, but for many years, my heart and mind were troubled by the idea of her virginity, the expectations of an unachievable purity that has for so long plagued the lives of mortal women. While I was infatuated with the paintings and sculptures she inspired, I was mostly indifferent to Mary as a figure in and of herself.

Quite suddenly, during a trip to Rome to meet a friend from New York, I became open to her significance for the first time. We visited St. Peter's Basilica, where I had my first encounter with Michelangelo's famous *Pietà*. Like so many, I was spellbound by the life-force of the sculpture. Struggling as I was then to achieve even a faithful rendering of proportion and light in my drawings at the academy where I was studying, one of my first thoughts was to marvel at how a twenty-four-year-old man could have hewn these figures in all their physical majesty and transcendent emotional truth, could have borne them into life. As if he knew that history might come to doubt the possibility that he had in fact—a mere youth, a mere mortal—created this *Pietà* of marble, or as if he needed to affirm to himself that he had, Michelangelo slipped into St. Peter's one night with a lantern to carve his signature in Latin across the bodice strap of Mary's robe: MICHAEL ANGELUS BONAROTUS FORENTINUE FACIEBA (Michelangelo Buonarroti, the Florentine, Made It). This was the only work he was ever to sign.

For me, few artistic creations I've seen equal the transsubstantial intensity of the *Pietà*—not even Rembrandt's great self-portrait that hangs in New York's Frick Museum, one of his last, where he, an old man, seems to be fractalizing, dissolving into the mysterious liquid light from which most of his other portraits emerge.

In the *Pietà*, two figures are carved as one into a pyramidal-shaped block of bone-pale marble—Christ, already departed from the earth, the stigmata of the crucifixion in his hands and feet, his subtle smile, and the Virgin Mary, gathering his dead-weight body to her broad bosom, face younger than Christ's, fully alive, the essence of grief itself. A smile not of happiness is perceptible on her face, a smile of some otherness that transforms what any mother who loses her son must experience, elevated into a state that is no longer simple loss or suffering. She stands at the door to one of the great mysteries of human existence: That which lives must die, and that which dies finds its way to life.

So this is how it is? she seemed to say to me. *So this is how it was to be?*

Mary has been depicted as hardly older than an adolescent, with a small, exquisitely beautiful face—aquiline nose, full lips, wide, almond-shaped eyes, perfection in the subtle bloom of fullness around her mouth and smooth forehead. While I often decry the idealization of women, I surprise myself in thinking that her youthful presence is perhaps necessary, a device through which

Michelangelo conflates past, present, and future. His Mary depicts at the heart of a woman the child who instinctively feels a connection to all living things and naturally expresses her empathy, she who carries the awesome biological destiny of bringing forth and nurturing life. In the *Pietà*, where Mary's visage is the age she would have been when visited by the angel Gabriel and her body that of the aging mother, a fully mature Christ dead on her lap, the whole narrative of Christ's existence is recorded in a glance; the entire cycle of life and death is felt in simultaneity.

"There are people who cannot stand beauty," Charles Cecil, an American painter in Florence, said in reference to Laszlo Toth and his 1972 assault on the *Pietà*. I wonder if it was not perhaps this very tenderness that he, Toth, could not stand, or if, in fact, beauty and tenderness are the same. Perhaps Mr. Toth simply brought the hammer down on that which broke his heart—chipping the eyelid, crushing the nose, and severing the arm of the Virgin because, well, because it is painful to stand in front of the *Pietà*. As I looked in at her through the bulletproof glass, isolated and protected deep within the chapel, she seemed lonely, bereft of the intimate proximity of viewers, sealed away in the *Capella del Crocifisso* since being reinstalled in 1973 after her restoration.

I know readers may feel that I saw in her merely an image of my own reality. But only a few days earlier, I had seen the *Mona Lisa* at the Louvre in Paris, the painting by Michelangelo's rival Leonardo da Vinci, and she, too, curiously enough, finds herself encased behind bulletproof glass, a rail separating her from the public, the only painting I know of in the Louvre that one cannot approach. The *Mona Lisa* appeared completely unmoved by her isolation, though—perhaps even to enjoy it, to revel in it, whereas Mary seemed stricken at being alone with her spiritual fullness, with her pity, compassion, and sorrow, with her "loyalty to the highest degree," as the Latin word *pietas*, with no direct translation into English, connotes. Her resonance, meant to radiate out into the far reaches of the world, was left instead to fill the sealed container of the chapel.

Tenderness, love, creativity, maternal care. . . . In the tumultuous world we inhabit, there could be nothing more welcome.

A few days before my visit to St. Peter's, the United States had invaded Iraq. In Florence and Rome, images of destruction dominated the media. As I looked at the *Pietà*, I remembered standing on a rooftop in New York, watching the second plane fly into the World Trade Center tower and was grieved, as I always am, by the memory of the people I saw falling like paper confetti to their deaths. I thought of articles I'd read over the years about the effects of the post-Gulf War embargo on the health and welfare of Iraqis, a story I'd read once about women who, having heard that supplies of medicine were forthcoming, waited with their eyes to the sky for planes that would never arrive to rescue their ailing children. What an awesome responsibility it would be if one were to side with nothing but life, nothing but love, nothing but creation: if we acted only to protect the living, our palms facing up.

For some reason still yet unknown to me today, for a long time after visiting the *Pietà* in Rome, I left off recording my thoughts. All that exists as a record of my trip are two ticket stubs: a bus ride in Rome taken at 9:56 in the morning and a ten-euro admission to the Vatican Museum. The pages from April and May comprise but few in my notebook.

Perhaps the *Pietà* was sinking into the depths of my unconscious, sinking into my days, I remaining silent as I made room for her monumental spirit. The first words to come again appeared in my journal, as follows:

The city is thinning out in the heat of July, tourists and exchange students moving on, Italians leaving early for August vacations. The smog has begun to lift, and for the first time in the ten harried months I have lived here, the community-oriented spirit of Italy has surfaced.

This morning, the young woman at the café prepared my standard order without asking what I wanted: cappuccino for me, café macchiato for my friend, acqua frizzante *for the two of us. Not wanting to snub her gesture of familiarity, I took my drinks out to where we typically enjoy them together under the shade of the canopy, though for the first time this week I was alone. When I got up to pay an hour later, I realized I'd left my wallet at home. She told me with a wave of her hand* "domani, domani"—*tomorrow, tomorrow, clearly not worried about the money.*

I passed two little bowls placed with care on the sidewalk, one filled with cat food, one with water, a piece of paper with a missing cat's picture, name, and age posted on the stone wall above.

In the café where a friend and I met early in the evening, the young wine steward, usually so cheerful, seemed troubled. He told us he was trying to decide whether or not to carry a particular vintage brought by a small, independent wine-maker for him to taste. The wine isn't very good, he said, but the man who made it is kind, sincere, devoted to his craft. With an air of melancholy, he asked if we would taste the wine and tell him what we thought. It seemed a little sour, we said, and he sighed in agreement, sorry to have to give the man the bad news.

I begin to sense the warp and weft of intersecting fates, the deep and complicated emotions that surround me. A bird lies dead on the side of the street, a middle-aged woman stooping over it to administer words of consolation. Two young children meet as their parents pause for a moment in passing. One reaches up to offer the other bread, the other reaches out to caress her cheek. I think as I watch them gazing into each other's faces that Leonardo must have witnessed just such a moment as this and used it to inform the rapt, hypnotic look he depicts between the Christ child and the young John in his "Madonna of the Rocks" in the Louvre.

As I walk through the park toward nightfall, the dust from the soccer field heaves forth in a dense wave, a group of teenage boys shouting out a choreography of play amid radiant shafts of the setting sun. The carousel is turning, faces of young children peering out from within. A young woman is riding around and around the circumference of the park on her bicycle, no older than fourteen, talking on her cell phone, hands hanging free of the handlebars. She passes me over and over again, first with an air of joyous freedom, then with gravity, and, finally, tears streaming down her face.

I approach another young woman sitting on a bench, neck arched, low-hanging head, intense concentration in the expression of her every gesture. I see that she is digging into her arm with a needle, the scratched-in scars all over her body a palimpsest of rage.

"Ah Bartleby! Ah life! . . ." Melville's words surface to me in the darkening dusk.

It is mid-July, and the days are already palpably shorter.

It is now, today, though, March 5, 2005, and I sit still looking out at the wind-swept graying horizon of Philadelphia. In many ways it is easier to destroy than to create, easier to give to the world the insults it seems to request rather than the heart it hopes to share. In answer to Gabriel's message, though the Virgin Mary affirmed an alternative and eternal message: Give birth to life, if only to our own, nurture that which we are called to give, and offer the fruits of our labor to the world.

14

courage

SAINT JOAN OF ARC

Oh Rouen, Rouen, must I die here,

and must you be my tomb?

Sᴛ. Jᴏᴀɴ ᴏꜰ Aʀᴄ

Jᴏᴀɴ ᴏꜰ Aʀᴄ ᴡᴀs ᴛʜᴇ ꜰɪʀsᴛ sᴀɪɴᴛ ᴡʜᴏ ᴇᴠᴇʀ ᴀᴘᴘᴇᴀʀᴇᴅ ᴛᴏ me, and her visitation had a profound effect on my life, establishing an ideal model against which I tested myself.

At the tender age of four I was moved by her story, which lay as I remembered it undisturbed in my conscious mind for over thirty years. I once tried to revisit her life when in my mid twenties, but was foiled by the clerk at the front desk of a Brooklyn branch of the New York Public Library, who couldn't find a single copy of the many transcripts of her trial said to be on hand. As if my orbit was to pass but once every decade within reach of her star, this missed opportunity would come to mean that my reencounter with Joan of Arc would be delayed until much later in my life. I wonder at times what would have happened had I asserted myself that summer evening and insisted that the clerk in the library try a little harder to find what I knew to be buried somewhere close at hand.

The question is a tantalizing one for me, in that each encounter I have had with Joan of Arc has heralded a dramatic shift in my relationship to the world. Perhaps, I thought, she eluded me that day in Brooklyn because it was not time yet for me to shed my treasured childhood idealizations. But from where I now sit writing on this cool early spring morning, borne to Philadelphia on the wings of fate, I think back on a similar spring day in Florence, Italy, now two years past, when I was to encounter my childhood guide for the second time. It was Friday afternoon, and I left the studio to walk down the Arno River and over the bridge to the British Library, hoping to find a good weekend read. It was one of the few times I'd be indulging in the luxury of words in the many months I'd been at the academy—a desire brought on by what I can only describe as a sudden "homesickness" for my first language, that of storytelling.

Having no preconceived notion about the book I sought, I decided to browse the stacks and select without question that which spoke to me first. I used to do this when I was young, and it seemed a fitting homage to years now past. Wandering through the elegant and spacious rooms on the main floor of the library, the vast windows overlooking the river, I descended to the voluminous stacks, pulling out books already familiar, books I'd always wanted to read, testing lines here and there to

mortal saints and immortal callings

see what caught my interest. Having led a life of reloca-
tion and migration from early childhood, I had found
libraries to be a sole nexus of experience to me—my
"hometown," as it were—the place to which I returned
in times of reexamination and reflection. This solitary
trip across the river, this foray from the world of drawing back into the world of words, was the closest I could
have come to returning to an old haunt. Memories from
as far back as I could remember began to surface as a soft
glow of nostalgia filled my thoughts.

When I saw the book that was to become mine that day
it was with the certainty befitting an encounter with an
old friend. I blew the dust off the top, cracking open the
arthritic spine of Vita Sackville West's *Saint Joan of Arc*,
printed on the dry and browning economy paper used in
England around the Second World War. The transcript of
Joan of Arc's trial sat next to it on the shelf. I read them
both, start to finish, that weekend, walking home, slow,
the biography open between my hands, stopping to read
it, in a café as it swelled with noise, returning home to
continue reading into the wee hours of the morning, just
as I'd done with books I'd loved as a child.

Sackville-West's biography starts out with the wonder,
magic, and miracle my youthful heart had desired to
remember well. A young, peasant girl, visited by the
archangel Michael, was directed to leave her home to
lead the French army to victory against the tyranny of
British rule. If she were to follow this command, she had
no choice but to deceive her parents, and, pretending to

visit the home of an uncle, she set out instead to speak to the dauphin, thus opening the door to what is surely one of the most mysterious extant stories of human destiny in the Western world.

Guided by St. Catherine of Alexandria and St. Margaret of Antioch, Joan picked the king from out of a crowd, having never seen him before. She divulged a secret that won his trust, sent her men to unearth a rusty sword that only she had known was buried behind the altar of a church, and led the French to what was considered an impossible victory at Orleans. Ushering the dauphin across France, she knelt by his side in the cathedral of Reims as he was anointed King Charles VII, consecrating her fame as the messenger of God and deliverer of France.

My memory of flickering black and white images matched well the narrative I now read of the first part of her life: horses and swords, battles and liberation, coronation and king, and the final tragedy of her martyr's death by flame. That which lay in the shadows, however, between the most miraculous events of her life, between the glory of her early victories and the tragedy of her death, were aspects of her life that I had either refused to remember or lacked the capacity to comprehend. I remembered nothing of the more human and corrupt anecdotes from what Vita Sackville West called the middle part of Joan's career, that which began when Charles VII distanced himself from her after his coronation. Quietly, he began to forge complicated liaisons behind her back and looked upon her as more of a nuisance than an aid, ignoring her pleas for money, soldiers, and arms that she might complete the overthrow of the British.

Through the doors of injustice, impelled by the will of God, Joan entered the domain of human power struggles, the invidious dehumanizing forces at the heart of human life that create their own systems, their own rules and regulations, functioning with viral stubbornness to ensure their continued hegemony. Saddened by what I imagined her life might have been, witnessing, as I read on, her isolation and powerlessness in the world of men, I watched her fall prey to the traps set through sophisticated political machinations.

Oblivious to the corruptions of greed and ignobility, Joan could not understand why she had been denied the resources to continue fighting when the mission to liberate France was not yet accomplished. With her command of the French regiments lifted, demoted to leading a small mercenary band, she faced one defeat after another. Eventually betrayed through a suspected act of treason toward her on the part of the French, she was captured and sold to the British, bounty toward the continued negotiations of boundaries and wealth between the upper echelons of warring dynasties.

Though I would normally not be surprised to encounter the traitorous underbelly of power, it came with both surprise and sorrow to me that the king of France may have betrayed her to England for his own personal gain. The transcendent power that had carried her across France would seem to have vanished—as if it had been but a dream from which she awoke to the nightmare of human tyranny.

Taken as a prisoner to Rouen, she was thrown into a dark cell, shackled in irons, and "guarded" by Englishmen "of the lowest rank." She was treated as any woman might who had been captured by enemy forces—both verbally and physically abused. Tried on unspecified charges, she faced dozens of interrogators, coldly rational licentiates of all sorts, doctors of theology and canon law in the pay of the British who were seeking one thing and one thing only—to find a reason, *any* reason, to burn her as a heretic.

Though the large architectural scaffolding of her trial recorded a voice that rang true and strong in answer to her prosecutors, a voice that had inspired generations of both men and women and filled my young heart with noble thoughts, I realized upon reading the specifics of her trial that, just as her life's activities, in general, contained the shadowy crevices of mortal failings, so her voice faltered at times, revealing the vulnerability, the fallibility, of the human heart and mind.

Perhaps it takes an empirical experience of the world, a personal experience of our eccentricities and weaknesses, to detect the fear creeping into her words, to understand the presence of doubt. She who had torn herself from family, endured the indecencies of clerical interrogation; she who had squared her shoulders to forceful opposition,

mortal saints and immortal callings

leading men in battle and sustaining injury; and she who had taken strength in the guiding wisdom of other-worldly figures, balked when St. Catherine divulged to her that it was part of her destiny to be captured. She admitted to her judges that if her voices had told her the specifics of when she was to be taken, she would not have "gone there."

I was dismayed to hear that my childhood hero had wavered when faced with the realization that she might die as a result of God's will in her life. Her judges seized at her inconsistency, asking: "So, if your voices had ordered you to sally forth from Compiègne, telling you that you would be captured, what would you have done?"

Had she known the hour, she said she would not have gone "willingly," and then she paused. "Just the same, I would have obeyed the command of the voices whatever was to happen." Hers must have been a confusing and tortured dilemma: She wanted to trust her voices but did not want to be imprisoned by the British; she wanted to trust God, but did not want to die.

And so it was that I began to understand Joan the myth was also Joan the maid—a peasant girl tortured by doubt and fear, horrified at the thought of being captured, terrified at the prospect of burning to death, no longer certain of the verity of her voices. On the one hand, they comforted her and "without them she'd be dead," but on the other hand, foreseeing what lay in store for her and losing faith in her strength to endure it, she faltered and began to question her instinct. She told her judges that Catherine had promised "help" but that she wasn't sure whether that help would come in the form of deliverance from prison or deliverance when she faced judgment. Had she hoped, then, even as they gathered the fuel for her pyre, that some thing or someone would intervene to set her free?

When the executioners arrived to take her to the imminent death that awaited her at the old marketplace square, she cried out pitiably, pulled at her hair, and lamented that she who was pure was to suffer such agony. Moments before she was raised above the pyre and tied to the stake, she turned to damn Pierre Cauchon, the man who had consigned her to the flames: "I will complain of you before God," she said.

Joan the Maid: She had in fact not rid France of the English, as I'd always believed, her role in their eventual expulsion deemed negligible by historians. Following her first spectacular military successes, she experienced a series of failures, as well, and thus was not nearly as brilliant a commander as I had always believed. She had not endured well the persecution of the English, nor embraced her death with the steadfastness my youth had demanded. She had not always followed the dictates of her voices, having leapt from a tower in defiance of their wish, and abjured before her judges their guidance in a last attempt to save herself.

mortal saints and immortal callings

What is it one understands as a child? The big archetypal play of light and dark, the details and subtleties of the human condition dormant within the innocence of our unformed selves. When I was a child, it was the mythic and heroic nature of Joan that captured my imagination, the transcendental magic of a girl who steals away from home, visited by angels and guided by saints, heavy-hearted to be leaving parents behind as she threw herself recklessly into the vicissitudes of war and politics, all at God's command. In the chaos of fire and night, she was clear-headed; in the dangers of battle, brave. She was to me the great warrior of justice, the white dove of peace, and she instilled in me the belief in our power to transcend all obstacles in the pursuit of what we feel we are called to do.

When, as a woman, I discovered Joan in irons, struggling to accept the fate she foresaw for herself, my first instinct was to abandon my childhood memories, to consider both myself naïve for having held to them so long, and Joan a less noble figure than I'd previously thought. As I pondered the contradictions between Joan the Maid and Joan the Warrior, though, I came to feel that our challenge as adults is to see the details of life not in isolation, but within the large turn of light and dark that guides our youth. As a child, I thought her invincible, for I understood that, metaphorically at least, her heart had not burned. As a woman, I understood that she was far more human than I could possibly have comprehended, her humanity yet another gift offered to us—a reminder that superhuman feats of courage spring from mortal hearts.

Upon studying the lives of saints in light of calling, we see, like the underlying structure of a symphony, similar movements repeating, loop after loop. An individual is pierced by a strong sense of the work they're to undertake. Some, as in the case of Joan of Arc, become aware of their calling through a dramatic supernatural encounter, but most, like Thérèse of Lisieux, simply "hear" a sure voice within or experience a growing sense of certainty about their destined path. For some, like Mother Teresa of Calcutta, the exact nature of what they're called to do may coalesce over time, evolving with experience. For still others, like Edith Stein, the nature of their work may unveil itself through grace.

In one way or another, the saints break with the past in order to pursue their future. As the life of Loyola so poignantly demonstrates—when his brother, guiding him through the rooms of the family estate, begged him to reconsider what he was leaving behind to pursue his new life—embracing one's true calling often requires leaving family and friends behind. It may also, as many saints have written, demand breaking down habitual patterns and responses to the world—banishing egotism, enfolding a greater sense of humility, and taking our place as more charitable members of the human community.

Through struggle, sacrifice, failure, and temptation, they remain committed to their vocations but develop, like Vincent de Paul, a more acute sense of the importance of their work. Through a connection to larger social and spiritual worlds, their efforts become grounded in some Other, fueled by sources of inspiration that may otherwise be difficult, perhaps even impossible, to access. Friends stimulate growth and provide the moral support, competence grows with experience, periods of dryness and darkness are borne with grace.

If there is one overriding message in the vocational lives of the saints, though, it appears to me to be the following: To accomplish anything of value requires that we overcome, as Francis of Assisi did, our greatest fears; that we struggle, as Teresa of Ávila did, with our demons; and that we eventually surrender, as Vincent de Paul did, our egotistical claims to ambition, in service to efforts that benefit the greater good. In so doing, our vocations liberate us from lives in which our deepest convictions are compromised or altogether suspended, from lives in which we repeat patterns that keep us from fulfilling our purpose, from lives in which we accept injustice and brutality as a necessary means to an end, from lives in which we wait for perfect circumstances to arise.

AFTERWORD

As a final word, I would like to say that while these writings draw heavily from the lives of the Catholic saints, and as such often take us down narrow ascetic pathways, we would do well to look toward the figurative and metaphoric beauty of their lives, as well: to look toward them not so much as role models per se—where to live a life of beauty, inspiration, and divine will we must embrace the life of a religious, renounce our involvement with the material world, or walk the earth barefoot, draped in a sack of cloth—but that we look to them as the sometimes imperfect humans that they once were who through a devotion to kindness and generosity, the courage to love, and a compassion for those less fortunate, strived to make the world a better place.

ACKNOWLEDGMENTS

I would like to express warm thanks for the encouragement and support of many people, including Gundula Jacobs, Rae and Sanjay Kapur, Hilary Masters, John McGonigle, and Heather Phillips. A special thanks to Lynn Sherwood for her positive presence and to the people in Les Cerqueux Sous Passavant, France, who extended their kind hospitality during the time that much of this book was written.

I would also like to offer my sincerest appreciation to those who so generously shared the details of their own devotions to the saints with me, inspiring me with their deep and profound lives of faith, including the Little Brothers of the Gospel in Brooklyn, New York; the Little Sisters of Jesus in Paterson, New Jersey; and my fellow pilgrims on the way to Santiago de Compostela in Spain.

The essay *Mortal Saints and Immortal Callings* was first published in the spring 2003 *Ruminator Review*, and I thank the *Ruminator* for permission to use it in this collection, as well as Matt Konrad for asking me to submit to their "Saints and Sinners" issue at the last minute.

And, finally, I am grateful to Lil Copan and Paraclete Press for the opportunity to publish this book.

notes

1 It's important to mention that this is not to imply that Edith Stein encountered a moment of grace because she was to convert to Catholicism; rather, it is to suggest that she encountered a moment of grace because she experienced an *illuminating moment* that, in her case, was to inform the direction of her vocation. The understanding of grace as the presence of the divine in the lives of people and in the history of the world exists in all religions.

2 Between 1378 and 1417 the Roman Papacy was challenged by antipopes.

3 Father Michael Di Gregorio, OSA, rector of the National Shrine of Saint Rita of Cascia in Philadelphia, believes that Rita's husband has been unfairly maligned. In his book *The Precious Pearl: The Story of Saint Rita of Cascia*, he suggests the depiction of her husband as a "violent" and "unfaithful" spouse rests upon a misinterpretation of an inscription on her casket.

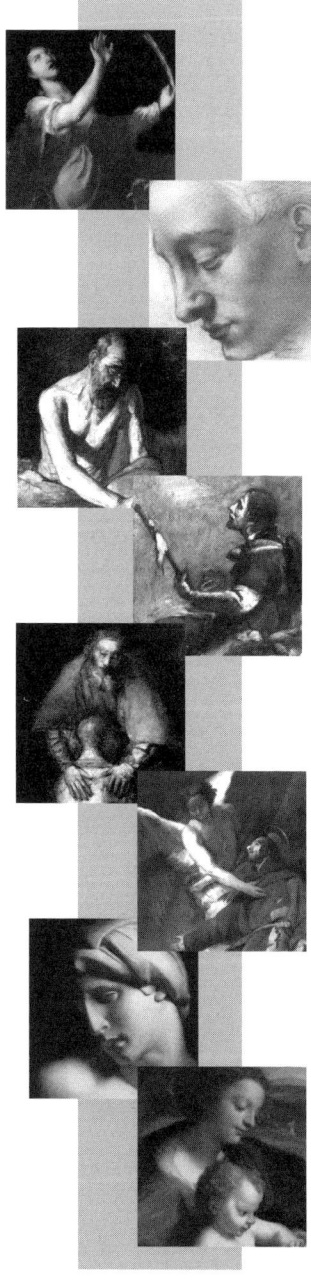

credits and sources

1: SAINT JOAN OF ARC AND SAINT MARGARET OF ANTIOCH

An earlier version of this essay was originally published in *Ruminator Review*, Spring 2003, and is reprinted with permission.

Reames, Sherry L., ed., *Middle English Legends of Women Saints* (Middle English Texts Series). Kalamazoo, MI: Medieval Institute Publications, 2003. The anonymous "Stanzaic Life of Margaret" is available in this book or on-line at http://www.teamsmedieval.org/texts/index.html.

Sackville-West, V., *Saint Joan of Arc*, Garden City, NJ: Country Life Press, 1936.

2: SAINT FRANCIS OF ASSISI

Bonaventure, *The Life of Francis*, trans. Ewert Cousins New York: HarperSanFrancisco, 2005. (Original translation published by Paulist Press, 1978.)

Chesterton, G. K., *Saint Francis of Assisi*. New York: Image, Doubleday, 1957.

Kazantzakis, Nikos, *Saint Francis, a Novel*, trans. P. A. Bien. New York: Simon & Schuster, 1962.

3: SAINT TERESA OF ÁVILA

Day, Dorothy, *From Union Square to Rome.* (http://www.catholicworker.org/dorothyday/daytext.cfm?TextID=2)

Peers, E. Allison, ed., *Complete Works of Teresa* (3 volumes). London: Sheed and Ward, 1944.

4: FRA ANGELICO

Guillaud, Jacqueline and Maurice, *Fra Angelico: The Light of the Soul.* New York: Clarkson N. Potter, Inc., 1986.

Hood, William, *Fra Angelico at San Marco.* New Haven, CT, and London: Yale University Press, 1993.

Vasari, Giorgio, *The Lives of the Artists*, trans. Julia Conaway. Oxford and New York: Oxford University Press, 1991.

5: HILDEGARD OF BINGEN, MOTHER TERESA, AND SAINT AGNES

Ellsberg, Robert, *All Saints, Daily Reflections on Saints, Prophets, and Witnesses for Our Time.* New York: Crossroad Publishing Company, 1997.

Pernoud, Régine, *Hildegard of Bingen*, trans. Paul Duggan. New York: Marlowe & Company, 1998.

Sebba, Anne, *Mother Teresa, Beyond the Image.* New York: Doubleday, 1997.

6: SAINT AUGUSTINE OF HIPPO

Augustine, *Confessions*, trans. Henry Chadwick. Oxford: Oxford University Press, 1991.

7: SAINT THÉRÈSE OF LISIEUX

Martin, Celine, *My Sister Saint Thérèse*. Rockford, IL: Tan Books and Publishers, 1997.

Saint Thérèse de Lisieux, *The Story of a Soul*, trans. John Beevers. New York: Image, Doubleday, 2001.

8: SAINTS BERNADETTE SOUBIROUS AND EDITH STEIN

Gaboriau, Florent, *The Conversion of Edith Stein*, trans. Ralph McInerny. South Bend, IN: Augustine's Press, 2002.

Ravier, André, *Bernadette*. Glasgow: Williams Collins Sons & Co. Ltd., 1979.

Stein, Edith, *Life in a Jewish Family*, trans. Josephine Koeppel, OCD. Washington, D.C.: ICS Publications, 1986.

9: SAINT IGNATIUS LOYOLA AND THE OTHER MATURE SAINTS

Ignatius of Loyola, *Personal Writings*, trans. Joseph A. Munitiz and Philip Endean. London: Penguin Books, 1996.

10: CHARLES DE FOUCAULD

de Foucauld, Charles: *Writings Selected with an Introduction by Robert Ellsburg*. Maryknoll, NY: Orbis Books, 1999.

11: SAINT RITA OF CASCIA

Di Gregorio, Michael, OSA, *The Precious Pearl: The Story of Saint Rita of Cascia*. Staten Island, NY: St. Pauls, 2003.

12: SAINT MICHAEL

Butler, Alban, *Butler's Lives of the Saints*. New York: P. J. Kenedy & Sons, 1956.

13: THE VIRGIN MARY

Garcia, Laura, "Edith Stein—Convert, Nun, Martyr." *Crisis* 15, no. 6 (June 1997): 32–35.

Stein, Edith, *Essays on Woman*, trans. Freda Mary Oben, Ph.D. Washington, DC: ICS Publications, 1987. (This is the second volume of *The Collected Works of Edith Stein*.)

14: SAINT JOAN OF ARC

Sackville-West, V., *Saint Joan of Arc*. Garden City, NY: Country Life Press, 1936.

The frontispiece and the art work at the beginning of each chapter have been reproduced from original paintings by the author.

selected bibliography

Augustine, *Confessions*, trans. Henry Chadwick. Oxford: Oxford University Press, 1991.

Barrett, W. P., ed. and trans., *The Trial of Jeanne d'Arc*. New York: Gotham House, 1932.

Bonaventure, *The Life of Francis*, trans. Ewert Cousins. HarperSanFrancisco, 2005. (Original translation published by Paulist Press, 1978).

Butler, Alban, *Butler's Lives of the Saints*. New York: P. J. Kenedy & Sons, 1956.

Calvet, J., *Louise de Marillac: a Portrait*, trans. G. F. Pullen. New York: P. J. Kenedy & Sons, 1959.

Carretto, Carlo, *Letters from the Desert*, trans. Rose Mary Hancock. Maryknoll, NY: Orbis Books, 2002.

Catherine of Siena, *The Dialogue*, trans. Suzanne Noffke, OP. Mahwah, NJ: Paulist Press, 1980.

Chesterton, G. K., *Saint Francis of Assisi*. New York: Image, Doubleday, 1957.

de Foucauld, Charles, *Writings Selected with an Introduction by Robert Ellsburg*. Maryknoll, NY: Orbis Books, 1999.

de Voraigne, Jacobus, *The Golden Legend; or, Lives of the Saints*, trans. William Caxton. London: J. M. Dent and Co., 1900.

Di Gregorio, Michael, OSA, *The Precious Pearl: The Story of Saint Rita of Cascia*. Staten Island, NY: St. Pauls, 2003.

Ellsberg, Robert, *All Saints, Daily Reflections on Saints, Prophets, and Witnesses for Our Time*. New York: Crossroad Publishing Company, 1997.

France, Peter, *Hermits: The Insights of Solitude*. New York: Martin's Griffin, 1996.

Gaboriau, Florent, *The Conversion of Edith Stein*, trans. Ralph McInerny. South Bend, IN: Augustine's Press, 2002.

Giordani, Igino, *Vincent de Paul: Servant of the Poor*, trans. Thomas J. Tobin. Milwaukee, WI: Bruce Publishing Company, 1961.

Guillaud, Jacqueline and Maurice, *Fra Angelico: The Light of the Soul*. New York: Clarkson N. Potter, Inc., 1986.

Hood, William, *Fra Angelico at San Marco*. New Haven, CT, and London: Yale University Press, 1993.

Hupka, Robert, *Michelangelo: Pietà*. Angers, France: Editions Arstella, 2003.

Ignatius of Loyola, *Personal Writings*, trans. Joseph A. Munitiz and Philip Endean. London: Penguin Books, 1996.

mortal saints and immortal callings

Jung, C. G., *Memories, Dreams, Reflections*, trans. Richard and Clara Winston. New York: Pantheon Books, a Division of Random House, 1961.

Kazantzakis, Nikos, *Saint Francis, a Novel*, trans. P. A. Bien. New York: Simon & Schuster, 1962.

Lazzeri, Zeffirino, ed., *The Little Flowers of Saint Francis*, trans. C. D. Tassinari. Florence: Giannini & Sons Publishers, 1926.

The Little Brothers and Little Sisters of Jesus, *Cry the Gospel With Your Life*. Denville, NJ: Dimension Books, Inc.

Martin, Celine, *My Sister Saint Thérèse*. Rockford, IL: Tan Books and Publishers, 1997.

McBrien, Richard P., *Lives of the Saints*. New York: HarperCollins, 2003.

Merad, Ali, *Christian Hermit In an Islamic World: A Muslim's View of Charles de Foucauld*, trans. Zoe Hersov. New York/Mahwah, NJ: Paulist Press, 1999.

Peers, E. Allison, ed., *Complete Works of St. Teresa* (3 volumes). London: Sheed and Ward, 1944.

Peri, Vittorio, *Rita of Cascia: Priceless Pearl of Umbria*, trans. Matthew J. O'Connell. Gorle (Bg): Editrice Velar, 1995.

Pernoud, Régine, *Hildegard of Bingen*, trans. Paul Duggan. New York: Marlowe & Company, 1998.

Pernoud, Régine and Marie-Véronique Clin, *Joan of Arc, Her Story*, revised and translated by Jeremy Duquesnay Adams. New York: St. Martin's Press, 1998.

Ravier, André, *Bernadette*. Glasgow: Williams Collins Sons & Co. Ltd., 1979.

Reames, Sherry L., ed., *Middle English Legends of Women Saints* (Middle English Texts Series). Kalamazoo, MI: Medieval Institute Publications, 2003.

Ryan, Frances, DC, and John E. Rybolt, CM, editors, *Vincent de Paul & Louise de Marillac: Rules, Conferences, and Writings*. New York: Paulist Press, 1995.

Sackville-West, V., *The Eagle and the Dove, A Study in Contrasts*. London: Michael Joseph Ltd., 1943.

Sackville-West, V., *Saint Joan of Arc*. Garden City, NY: Country Life Press, 1936.

Sebba, Anne, *Mother Teresa, Beyond the Image*. New York: Doubleday, 1997.

Six, Jean-François, *The Spiritual Autobiography of Charles de Foucauld*, trans. J. Holland Smith. Ijamsville, MD: The Word Among Us, 2003.

Stein, Edith, *Essays on Woman*, trans. Freda Mary Oben, Ph.D. Washington, DC: ICS Publications, 1987. (This is the second volume of *The Collected Works of Edith Stein*.)

Stein, Edith, *Life in a Jewish Family*, trans. Josephine Koeppel, OCD. Washington, D.C.: ICS Publications, 1986.

Taylor, Therese, *Bernadette of Lourdes: Her Life, Death, and Visions*. London and New York: Burns & Oates, a Continuum International Publishing Group Imprint, 2003.

Teresa of Ávila, *The Life of Saint Teresa of Ávila by Herself*, trans. J. M. Cohen. London: Penguin Books, 1957.

Saint Thérèse de Lisieux, *The Story of a Soul*, trans. John Beevers. New York: Image, Doubleday, 2001.

Trask, Willard, compiler and translator, *Joan of Arc: In Her Own Words*. New York: Books & Co., a Turtle Point Imprint, 1996.

Vasari, Giorgio, *The Lives of the Artists*, trans. Julia Conaway. Oxford and New York: Oxford University Press, 1991.

About Paraclete Press

Who We Are

Paraclete Press is an ecumenical publisher of books on Christian spirituality for people of all denominations and backgrounds.

We publish books that represent the wide spectrum of Christian belief and practice—from Catholic to Evangelical to liturgical to Orthodox.

We market our books primarily through booksellers; we are what is called a "trade" publisher, which means that we like it best when readers buy our books from booksellers, our partners in successfully reaching as wide an audience as possible.

Paraclete Press is the publishing arm of the Community of Jesus, an ecumenical monastic community in the Benedictine tradition. We are uniquely positioned in the marketplace without connection to a large corporation or conglomerate and with informal relationships to many branches and denominations of faith. We focus on publishing a diversity of thoughts and perspectives—the fruit of our diversity as a company.

What We Are Doing

Paraclete Press is publishing books that show the diversity and depth of what it means to be Christian. We publish books that reflect the Christian experience across many cultures, time periods, and houses of worship.

We publish books about spiritual practice, history, ideas, customs, and rituals, and books that nourish the vibrant life of the church.

We have several different series of books within Paraclete Press, including the bestselling Living Library series of modernized classic texts, A Voice from the Monastery—giving voice to men and women monastics on what it means to live a spiritual life today, and Many Mansions—for exploring the riches of the world's religious traditions and discovering how other faiths inform Christian thought and practice.

Learn more about us at our Web site:
www.paracletepress.com, or call us toll-free at
800- 451-5006.